Biology

W!

11–14

Biology NOW! 11–14

Peter D Riley

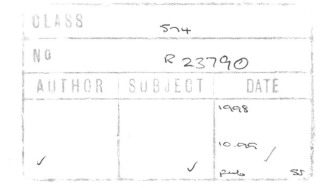

JOHN MURRAY

Titles in this series:
Biology Now! 11–14 Pupil's Book   ISBN 0 7195 7548 6
Biology Now! 11–14 Teacher's Resource Book   ISBN 0 7195 7549 4
Chemistry Now! 11–14 Pupil's Book   ISBN 0 7195 7546 X
Chemistry Now! 11–14 Teacher's Resource Book   ISBN 0 7195 7547 8
Physics Now! 11–14 Pupil's Book   ISBN 0 7195 7544 3
Physics Now! 11–14 Teacher's Resource Book   ISBN 0 7195 7545 1

First published in 1998
by John Murray (Publishers) Ltd
50 Albemarle Street
London W1X 4BD

Layouts by Black Dog Design
Artwork by Mike Humphries, Linden Artists,
Jeff Edwards and Richard Duszczak
Cover design by John Townson/Creation

Typeset in 12/14pt Garamond by Wearset, Boldon,
Tyne and Wear
Printed and bound by G. Canale, Italy

A catalogue entry for this title is available from the
British Library

ISBN 0 7195 7548 6

Contents

Preface

To the pupil

Biology is the scientific study of living things. It includes investigations on tiny structures, such as cells, and to huge structures, such as a rainforest, ocean or even the whole Earth! Some biologists are even looking for signs of life in other parts of the Solar System or on planets around other stars.

Our knowledge of biology has developed from the observations, investigations and ideas of many people over a long period of time. Today this knowledge is increasing more rapidly as there are more biologists – people who study living things – than ever before.

In the past, few people other than scientists were informed about the latest discoveries. Today, through newspapers and television, everyone can learn about the latest discoveries on a wide range of biological topics, from curing illnesses and developing new foods to ways of reducing environmental damage and conserving rare species.

Biology Now! 11–14 covers the requirements of your examinations in a way that I hope will help you understand how observations, investigations and ideas have led to the scientific facts we use today. The questions are set to help you extract information from what you read and see, and to help you think more deeply about each chapter in this book. Some questions are set so you can discuss your ideas with others and develop a point of view on different scientific issues. This should help you in the future when new scientific issues, which are as yet unknown, affect you life.

The scientific activities of thinking up ideas to test and carrying out investigations are enjoyed so much by many people that they take up a career in science. Perhaps *Biology Now! 11–14* may help you to take up a career in science too.

To the teacher

Biology Now! 11–14 has been written to cover the requirements of the curriculum for the Common Entrance Examination at 13+, the National Curriculum for Science at Key Stage 3 and equivalent junior courses. It aims to help pupils to become more scientifically literate by encouraging them to examine the information in the text and illustrations in order to answer questions about it in a variety of ways. The book presents science as a human activity by considering the development of scientific ideas from the earliest times to present day, and deals with applications of scientific knowledge and issues that arise from them.

Biology Now! 11–14 and its supporting *Teacher's Resource Book* are designed to provide the biology content of a balanced science course in which biology, chemistry and physics are taught separately. It may also be used as a supplementary text in more integrated courses to demonstrate aspects of science as a human activity and to extend skills in comprehension.

Acknowledgements

I would like to thank Sarah Corps for reading and advising on the manuscript, and Katie Mackenzie Stuart and Julie Jones for their encouragement, help and support throughout the preparation of this book.

The following have kindly given permission for artwork/tables to be reproduced or adapted:

Table 2.5 (**p. 22**), from *Biology in Action* by D. Luxton. © Kluwer Academic & Lipincott-Raven Publishers incorporating Chapman & Hall and Rapid Science and Blackie.
Tables 2.6 & 2.7 (**p. 24**) from AJ Churchill, *School Science Review* June 1994, **75** (273).
Figure A (**p. 108**) from *Green Inheritance* by Anthony Huxley. © Gaia Books Ltd.
Figure 7.11 (**p. 113**) from PW Freeland, *School Science Review* September 1977, Biology notes, p. 59.
Table 8.1 (**p. 132**) from PW Freeland, *School Science Review* December 1981, Biology notes, p. 278.
Table 10.1 (**p. 167**) from JM Cooper, *School Science Review* March 1993, **74** (268).
Table 11.2 (**p. 198**) from PM Durrant, *School Science Review* September 1979, Biology Notes, p. 68.
Figures 11.28 (**p. 199**), 11.29 (**p. 200**) & 11.30 (**p. 200**) from JW Cox, *School Science Review*, September 1974, Biology Notes, pp. 85 & 86.

The following have supplied photographs or have given permission for photographs to be reproduced:

Cover Eye of Science/Science Photo Library; **p.1** *clockwise from top* Heather Angel, Heather Angel, Gerard Lacz/NHPA; **p.5** J.C. Revy/Science Photo Library; **p.10** G.I. Bernard/NHPA; **p.14** Andrew Lambert; **p.16** John Townson/Creation; **p.17** Biophoto Associates/Science Photo Library; **p.19** Heather Angel; **p.27** *top* Royal College of Physicians Photo Library, *bottom* Jason Venus/Biofotos; **p.42** Klaus Guldbrandsen/Science Photo Library; **p.49** Biophoto Associates/Science Photo Library; **p.53** Wellcome Institute Library, London; **p.55** The Stock Market Photo Agency Inc.; **p.57** Damien Lovegrove/Science Photo Library; **p.60** Caroline Penn/Water Aid; **p.61** Anglian Water Services Ltd; **p.62** *top* ©1997 Cheryl Hogue/Ancient Art & Architecture Collection, *bottom* Bruce Paton/Panos Pictures; **p.66** ©The Trustee of the Wellcome Trust/National Medical Slide Bank; **p.68** Tim Beddow/Science Photo Library; **p.69** Medical Illustration Services/Glasgow Royal Infirmary University NHS Trust; **p.70** John Durham/Science Photo Library; **p.71** Mary Evans Picture Library; **p.73** Deep Light Productions/Science Photo Library; **p.76** John Townson/Creation; **p.77** Courtesy of the Health Education Authority; **p.79** S.I.U. School of Medicine/Science Photo Library; **p.80** Andrew Lambert; **p.81** ©Bubbles/John Garrett; **p.85** The Stock Market Photo Agency Inc.; **p.86** CNRI/Science Photo Library; **p.87** Motta & Familiari/Anatomy Dept/University "La Sapienza", Rome/Science Photo Library; **p.88** *left* Tim Beddow/Science Photo Library, *right* Hank Morgan/Science Photo Library; **p.89** *left* Sally Greenhill © Sally & Richard Greenhill, *right* Andrew Lambert; **p.93** Stevie Grand/Science Photo Library; **p.95** *from top* John Townson/Creation, John Townson/Creation, Last Resort Picture Library, Saturn Stills/Science Photo Library, Last Resort Picture Library; **p.96** Sally Greenhill © Sally and Richard Greenhill; **p.99** Heather Angel; **p.104** Harry Smith Horticultural Photographic Collection; **p.107** Stefan Meyers/Ardea London Ltd; **p.108** ©Juliet Hignet/Hutchison Library; **p.109** *all* Nigel Cattlin/Holt Studios International; **p.115** Heather Angel; **p.116** *top* Oxford Scientific Films/Geoff Kidd, *bottom* ©Garden Matters; **p.118** *all* Eye of Science/Science Photo Library; **p.120** Stephen Dalton/NHPA; **p.121** *all* Stephen Dalton/NHPA *except middle left* Oxford Scientific Films/Dr J.A.L. Cooke; **p.122** *from top* ©Wildlife Matters, Paul Simons/Biofotos, Harry Smith Horticultural Photographic Collection; **p.131** John Howard/Science Photo Library; **p.134** Planet Earth Pictures/Andre Bartschi; **p.135** ©Breck P. Kent/Earth Scenes/Oxford Scientific Films; **p.139** *a* A.N.T./NHPA, *b* ©Michele Hall/Oxford Scientific Films, *c* Jeff Foott Productions/Bruce Coleman Ltd; **p.142** *top* ©Derek Whitford, *bottom* ©David Woodfall/NHPA; **p.145** Heather Angel; **p.146** Planet Earth Pictures/Verena Tunnicliffe; **p.152** *from left* Heather Angel, Andrew Henley/Biofotos, Jany Sauvanet/NHPA; **p.153** Sally Greenhill © Sally and Richard Greenhill; **p.157** M.I. Walker/Science Photo Library; **p.158** Manfred Kage/Science Photo Library; **p.159** Harry Smith Horticultural Photographic Collection; **p.161** Associated Press; **p.162** Simon Fraser/Science Photo Library; **p.163** *left* Bob Gibbons/Holt Studios International, *right* Nigel Cattlin/Holt Studios International; **p.164** *both* Mary Evans Picture Library; **p.166** P.H. Plailly/Eurelios/Science Photo Library; **p.168** David Woodfall/NHPA; **p.169** Harwood/Ecoscene; **p.170** Sally Morgan/Ecoscene; **p.171** ©Jacomina Wakeford/ICCE; **p.177** David Woodfall/NHPA; **p.178** *top* John Hawkins/Frank Lane Picture Agency, *bottom* Stephen Dalton/NHPA; **p.179** *left* Planet Earth Pictures © Neil McIntyre, *right* Allan G. Potts/Bruce Coleman Ltd; **p.182** *top* Heather Angel, *bottom* G.I. Bernard/NHPA; **p.186** Alexandra Jones/Ecoscene; **p.187** *top* ©Garden & Wildlife Matters, *bottom* John Mason/Ardea London Ltd; **p.189** ©Richard Davies/Oxford Scientific Films; **p.193** ©Wildlife Matters; **p.195** A.N.T./NHPA; **p.196** *left* US Geological Survey/Science Photo Library, *right* Copyright 1995, Worldsat International and J. Knighton/Science Photo Library.

(*b* = bottom, *c* = centre, *l* = left, *r* = right, *t* = top)

The publishers have made every effort to contact copyright holders. If any have been overlooked they will make the necessary arrangements at the earliest opportunity.

1 The structure of living things

Figure 1.1 There is a great variety in the structure of living things, as these photographs show.

Organs and organ systems

Biology is the study of living things. The parts of a body that perform tasks to keep a living thing alive are called organs and most organs work together in groups called organ systems.

Organ systems of a human

There are ten organ systems in the human body. They are listed below but will be covered in more detail later in the book. The tasks they carry out are sometimes called life processes.

1 The **sensory system** is made up of sense organs such as the eye and the ear. The function of this system is to provide information about the surroundings.

1 Which organ system:
   a) transports materials around the body
   b) absorbs food into the blood
   c) detects changes in the environment
   d) produces hormones
   e) co-ordinates activities
   f) takes in oxygen from the air
   g) supports the body
   h) produces offspring
   i) removes wastes from the blood
   j) moves bones?

2 Which organ system or systems are involved in:
   a) movement
   b) nutrition
   c) circulation?

3 What other sense organs are in the sensory system?

4 What is the name of the hormone that makes your heart beat faster and directs more blood to your muscles?

5 What movements take place in the body that you do not have to think about?

2 The **nervous system** comprises the brain, spinal cord and nerves. This system controls the actions of the body and co-ordinates many of its activities without you having to think about them. For example, you breathe in and out automatically.

3 The **respiratory system** is located in the chest. It is formed by the windpipe, the lungs, the ribs and rib muscles (called the intercostal muscles) and the diaphragm. The system works to draw in air and then expel it. While in the lungs oxygen passes from the air into the blood and carbon dioxide passes from the blood into the air.

4 The **digestive system** is a long tube through the body in which food is broken down and absorbed into the blood. Two major parts of the digestive system are the stomach and the small intestine.

5 The **circulatory system** transports materials around the body in a liquid called the blood. The blood is moved by the pumping action of the heart along tubes called blood vessels.

6 The **excretory system** cleans waste from the blood by a filtration process in the kidneys. The liquid containing the waste is called urine. It is stored in the bladder before it is released.

7 The **skeletal system** is made up of 206 bones. They provide support for the body and have joints between them that help the body to move. Some bones form a protective structure, for example, the bones in the skull form a protective case around the brain.

8 The **muscle system** provides the mechanism for movement. A muscle is capable of making itself shorter to exert a pulling force on a bone.

9 The **endocrine system** is made up of glands which release chemicals called hormones into the blood. The adrenal gland is an example of an endocrine gland. It is found just above the kidney and releases (or secretes) a hormone called adrenaline. You feel the effect of adrenaline if you are asked to read aloud or act in front of a large audience, or take part in athletics. It makes your heart beat faster and directs more blood to your muscles.

10 The **reproductive system** of the male produces sperm cells and the reproductive system of the female produces eggs and provides a place for a baby to grow.

6 How does your pattern of breathing change when you exercise and then rest?

7 Write down the names of any bones that you know (without looking them up) and say where they are found in the body.

8 You are walking across a road and hear a sound behind you. You turn and see that a car has swerved to avoid a cat and is heading straight for you. What body systems work to get you out of the car's way? Why do you think these systems developed?

For discussion

Are there any organs or organ systems that a body could lose and still stay alive?

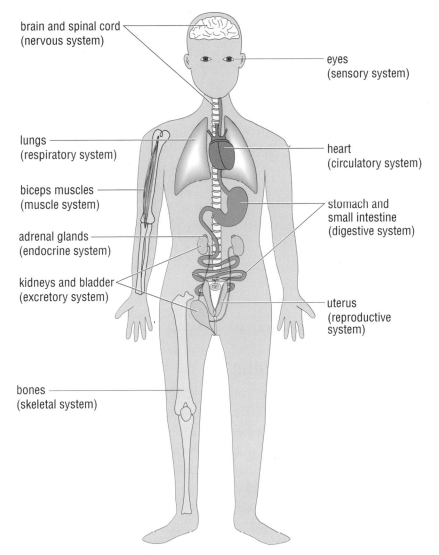

brain and spinal cord (nervous system)

eyes (sensory system)

lungs (respiratory system)

heart (circulatory system)

biceps muscles (muscle system)

stomach and small intestine (digestive system)

adrenal glands (endocrine system)

kidneys and bladder (excretory system)

uterus (reproductive system)

bones (skeletal system)

Figure 1.2 Organs of the human body.

Organs of a flowering plant

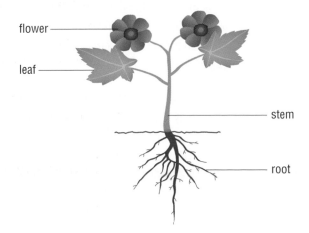

flower

leaf

stem

root

Figure 1.3 Organs of a flowering plant.

9 Draw a table featuring the organs of a flowering plant and the tasks they perform.

10 How is the leaf dependent on the root and the stem?

11 Which life processes or tasks do you think are found in both plants and humans? Explain your answer.

There are four main organs in the body of a flowering plant. They are the root, stem, leaf and flower. Each organ may be used for more than one task or life process.

1 The **root** anchors the plant and takes up water and minerals from the soil. The roots of some plants, such as the carrot, store food.

2 The **stem** transports water and food and supports the leaves and the flowers. Some plants, such as trees, store food in their stems.

3 The **leaf** produces food. In some plants, such as the onion, food is stored in the bases of the leaves. The swollen leaf bases make a bulb.

4 The **flower** contains the reproductive organs of the plant.

All the organs work together to keep the plant alive so that it can grow and produce offspring.

From organs to cells

Marie F. X. Bichat (1771–1802) was a French doctor who did many post mortems. In the last year of his life he carried out 600. He cut up the bodies of dead people to find out how they had died. From this he discovered that organs were made of layers of materials. He called these layers 'tissues' and identified 21 different kinds. For a while scientists thought that tissues were made of simple non-living materials.

In 1665, long before Bichat was born, an English scientist named Robert Hooke (1635–1703) used a microscope to investigate the structure of a very thin sheet of cork. He discovered that it had tiny compartments in it. He thought of them as rooms and called them 'cells', after the small rooms in monasteries where monks worked and meditated.

Bichat did not examine the tissues he had found under a microscope because most of those made at that time did not produce very clear images. When better microscopes were made, scientists investigated pieces of plants and found that, like cork, they also had a cell structure. The cells in Hooke's piece of cork had been empty but other plant cells were found to contain structures.

A Scottish scientist called Robert Brown (1773–1858) studied plant cells and noticed that each one had a dark spot inside it. In 1831 he named the spot the 'nucleus' which means 'little nut'.

Matthias Schleiden (1804–1881) was a German scientist who studied the parts of many plants. In 1838 he put forward a theory that all plants were made of cells. A year later Theodor Schwann, another German scientist, stated that animals were also made of cells.

The ideas of Schleiden and Schwann became known as the Cell Theory. It led other scientists to make more discoveries about cells and to show that tissues are made up of groups of similar cells.

1 Where did Bichat get his ideas that organs were made from tissues?

2 Who first described 'cells' and where did the idea for the word come from?

3 Who named the nucleus and what does it mean?

4 What instrument was essential for the study of cells?

5 How could the Cell Theory have been developed sooner?

6 Arrange these parts of a body in order of size starting with the largest: cell, organ, tissue, organ system.

Cells

There are ten times more cells in your body than there are people on the Earth. If you stay in the water a long time at a swimming pool you may notice that part of your skin sometimes flakes off when you dry yourself. These flakes are made of dead skin cells. You are losing skin cells all the time but in a much smaller way. As your clothes rub against your skin they pull off tiny flakes which pass into the air and settle in the dust. A small part of the dirt that cleaners sweep up at the end of a school day comes from the skin that the pupils have left behind.

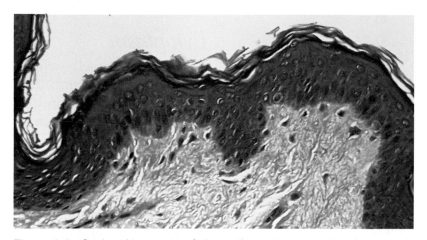

Figure 1.4   Section of human skin. Cells can be seen flaking off the surface.

Figure 1.4 shows a section of human skin that has been stained and photographed down a microscope using a high power objective lens. When unstained, the different parts of the cells are colourless and are difficult to distinguish. In the 1870s it was discovered that dyes could be made from coal tar which would stain different parts of the cell. Cell biologists found they could stain the nucleus and other parts of the cell different colours to see them more easily.

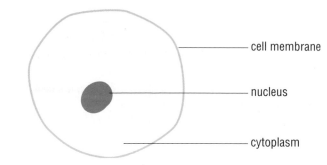

cell membrane

nucleus

cytoplasm

Figure 1.5   A typical animal cell.

12 Why are most specimens of cells stained before they are examined under the microscope?

13 You look down a microscope at a slide labelled 'Cells'. You can see a coloured substance with dots in it and lines that divide the substance into rectangular shapes. Inside the rectangular shapes, what are:
   a) the dots
   b) the lines
   c) the coloured substance?

14 How does the cell membrane protect the cell?

15 If there are about 6000 million people on the Earth, how many cells have you got in your body?

Basic parts of a cell

Nucleus

This is the control centre of the cell. It contains the genetic material, called DNA (its full name is deoxyribonucleic acid). The DNA molecule is a long chain of smaller molecules. They occur in different combinations along the DNA molecule. The combinations of molecules provide instructions for the cell to make chemicals to keep it alive or to build its cell parts. When a cell divides the DNA divides too, so that the nucleus of each new cell receives all the instructions to keep the new cell alive and enable it to grow.

Cytoplasm

This is a watery jelly which fills most of the cell in animal cells. It can move around inside the cell. The cytoplasm may contain stored food in the form of grains. Most of the chemical reactions that keep the cell alive take place in the cytoplasm.

Cell membrane

This covers the outside of the cell and has tiny holes in it called pores that control the movement of chemicals in or out of the cell. Dissolved substances such as food, oxygen and carbon dioxide can pass through the cell membrane. Some harmful chemicals are stopped from entering the cell by the membrane.

Parts found only in plant cells

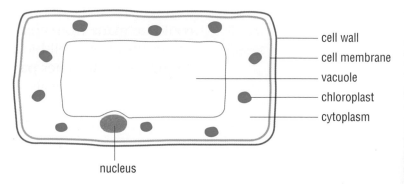

Figure 1.6 A typical plant cell.

Cell wall

This is found outside the membrane of a plant cell. It is made of cellulose which is a tough material that gives support to the cell.

Chloroplasts

These are found in the cytoplasm of many plant cells. They contain a green pigment called chlorophyll which traps a small amount of the energy in sunlight. This energy is used by the plant to make food in a process called photosynthesis (see Chapter 7). Chloroplasts are found in many leaf cells and in the stem cells of some plants.

Large vacuole

This large space in the cytoplasm of a plant cell is filled with a liquid called cell sap which contains dissolved sugars and salts. When the vacuole is full of cell sap the liquid pushes outwards on the cell wall and gives it support. If the plant is short of water, the support is lost and the plant wilts.

Some animal cells and Protoctistas (see page 144) have vacuoles but they are much smaller than those found in plant cells.

Adaptation in cells

The word adaptation means the change of an existing design for a particular task (see also page 175). The basic designs of plant and animal cells were shown in the last section, but many cells are adapted which allows them to perform a more specific task. Here are some common examples of the different types of plant and animal cells.

Root hair cells

These grow a short distance behind the root tip. The cells have long thin extensions that allow them to grow easily between the soil particles. The shape of these extensions gives the root hair cells a large surface area through which water can be taken up from the soil.

16 Name two things that give support to a plant cell.
17 Would you expect to find chloroplasts in a root cell? Explain your answer.
18 Why do plants wilt if they are not watered regularly?

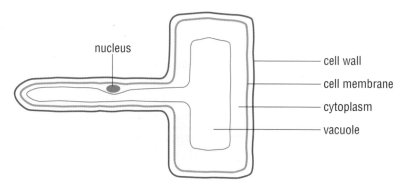

nucleus — cell wall — cell membrane — cytoplasm — vacuole

Figure 1.7 A root hair cell.

Palisade cells

These cells have a shape that allows them to pack closely together in the upper part of a leaf, near the light. They have large numbers of chloroplasts in them to trap as much light energy as possible.

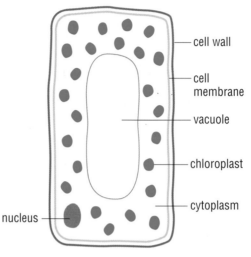

cell wall

cell membrane

vacuole

chloroplast

cytoplasm

nucleus

Figure 1.8 A palisade cell.

Ciliated epithelial cells

Cells that line the surface of structures are called epithelial cells. Cilia are microscopic hair-like extensions of the cytoplasm. If cells have one surface covered in cilia they are described as ciliated. Ciliated epithelial cells line the throat. Air entering the throat contains dust that becomes trapped in the mucus of the throat lining. The cilia wave to and fro and carry the dust trapped in the mucus away from the lungs.

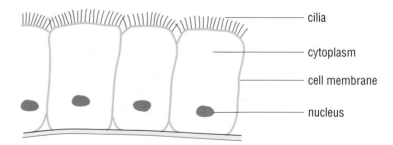

cilia

cytoplasm

cell membrane

nucleus

Figure 1.9 Ciliated epithelial cells.

Sperm cells

These transport the male genetic material in their nucleus. They have a stream-lined shape which allows them to move easily through the liquid as they travel towards the female egg. They have a tail that waves from side to side to push the cell forwards.

19 What changes have taken place in the basic plant cell to produce a root hair cell?

20 How is a palisade cell different from a root hair cell? Explain these differences.

21 Why would it be a problem if root hair cell extensions were short and stubby?

22 How are sperm and egg cells **a)** similar and **b)** different?

23 Smoking damages the cilia lining the breathing tubes. What effect might this have on breathing?

24 Why are there different kinds of cells?

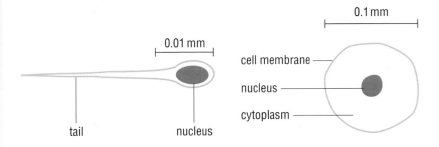

Figure 1.10   Sperm and egg cell (showing size scale).

Egg cells

These contain the female genetic material in their nucleus. They are much larger than sperm cells because they contain a food store and do not move on their own. When a sperm reaches an egg the genetic material from the sperm combines with that in the egg in a process called fertilisation. This produces a cell which divides many times to produce an embryo. The food and energy for early growth of the embryo is provided by the egg.

Making observations

When you make observations you look closely and with a purpose. For example, you may *look* at a plant and just see its flowers and leaves, but if you *observed* a plant you could study it to find out how the leaves and flowers are arranged on the stem. Leaves can be arranged in many ways, for example, they may grow alternately along a stem or they may be arranged in pairs. Flowers may be arranged singly or in columns.

B St John's wort

A Rosebay willow herb

25 How are the leaves arranged in plant A and plant B in Figure 1.11?

26 How are the flowers arranged in A and B?

Figure 1.11   The leaves and flowers in two plants.

Drawing specimens

Explorers of the 17th and 18th Centuries collected specimens of the plants and animals they found and brought them back to the scientists in Europe for further study. Many of the living things died during the journey and by the time they arrived their remains were decayed and of little use to the scientists. Even when the specimens were kept in a preservative their colours would be lost or some other feature would change. To solve the problem of showing how these living things appeared in their habitats, artists accompanied the explorers and drew pictures of the plants and animals that were discovered. The scientists back in Europe could then use both the specimens and the pictures to help them study and classify the new living things that were being discovered.

1 Why were artists taken on explorations in the 17th and 18th Centuries?

2 Why do you think artists are used much less in expeditions today?

3 Why might an organism be drawn ×5? Give an example. Why might another organism be drawn ×½? Give an example.

4 What is the true size of the living things in these drawings?

Figure A   17th Century biological drawing.

Biological drawings of specimens are still made today. The size of the specimen is usually indicated in one of two ways. A line may be drawn next to the picture to indicate the length of the specimen, or the drawing may have ×5 or ×½ next to it. The × symbol means times larger or smaller; the number gives an indication of the size. For example, ×5 means the drawing is five times larger than the specimen, and ×½ means the drawing is half the size of the specimen.

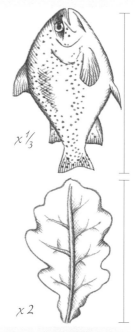

Figure B   A leaf and a fish.

Microscope

A microscope is used for looking at specimens very closely. Most laboratory microscopes give a magnification up to about 200 times but some can give a magnification of over a 1000 times. The microscope must also provide a clear view and this is achieved by controlling the amount of light shining onto the specimen.

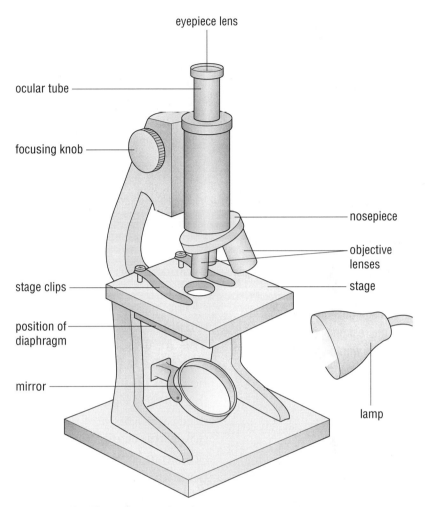

Figure 1.12 The main parts of a microscope.

Light is collected by a mirror at the base of the microscope. The mirror is held in special joints that allow it to move in any direction. The light comes from a lamp or from a sunless sky. It must never be collected directly from the Sun as this can cause severe eye damage and blindness. Some microscopes have a built-in lamp instead of a mirror. The light either shines directly through a hole in the stage onto the specimen or it passes through a hole in a diaphragm. The diaphragm allows the amount of light reaching the specimen to be controlled by increasing or decreasing the size of the hole. The light shining through a specimen is called transmitted light.

Above the specimen is the ocular tube. This has an eyepiece lens at the top and one or more objective lenses at the bottom. The magnification of the two lenses is written on them. An eyepiece lens may give a magnification of ×5 or ×10. An objective lens may give a

27 What is a microscope used for?

28 What advice would you give someone about how to collect light to shine into a microscope?

29 What magnification would you get by using an eyepiece of ×5 magnification with an objective lens of ×10 magnification?

30 If you had a microscope with ×5 and ×10 eyepieces and objective lens of ×10, 15 and 20, what powers of magnification could your microscope provide?

31 How would you advise someone to use the three objective lenses on the nosepiece?

32 Why should you not look down the microscope all the time as you try to focus the specimen?

33 Look at the picture of the microscope on page 11 and describe the path taken by light from a lamp near the microscope to the eye.

magnification of ×10, 15 or 20. The magnification provided by both the eyepiece lens and the objective lens is found by multiplying their magnifying powers together. Most microscopes have three objective lenses on a nosepiece at the bottom of the ocular tube. The nosepiece can be rotated to bring each objective lens under the ocular tube in turn. An investigation with the microscope always starts by using the lowest power objective lens then working up to the highest power objective lens if it is required.

A specimen for viewing under the microscope must be put on a glass slide. The slide is put on the stage and held in place by the stage clips. The slide should be positioned so that the specimen is in the centre of the hole in the stage.

The view of the specimen is brought into focus by turning the focusing knob on the side of the microscope. This may raise or lower the ocular tube or it may raise or lower the stage on which the slide of the specimen is held. In either case you should watch from the side of the microscope as you turn the knob to bring the objective lens and specimen close together. If you looked down the ocular tube as you did this you might crash the objective lens into the specimen which could damage both the lens and the specimen. When the objective lens and the specimen are close together, but not touching, look down the eyepiece and turn the focusing knob so that the objective lens and specimen move apart. If you do this slowly, the blurred image will become clear.

Finding the size of microscopic specimens

The disc of light you see when you look down a microscope is called the field of view. You can estimate the size of the specimens you see under the microscope if you know the size of the field of view. A simple way to find the size of the field of view is to put a piece of graph paper on a slide and examine it using the low power objective lens. The squares on the graph should be 1 mm across. Microscopic measurements are not made in millimetres. They are measured in micrometres. 1 mm = 1000 micrometres (written as 1000 μm).

If the field of view is two squares across it has a diameter of 2000 μm. If you remove the slide with the graph paper and replace it with a slide with some soil particles, you could estimate the size of a soil particle by judging how far it crosses the field of view.

34 A field of view was found to be 2000 µm in diameter. A soil particle reached one quarter of the way across it. How long would you estimate the length of the particle to be?

35 The fields of view of three lenses were measured. A was 100 µm, B was 3000 µm and C was 500 µm. Which was the most powerful lens and which was the least powerful lens?

36 Why does the field of view decrease as the power of the objective lens increases?

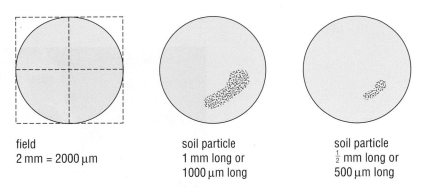

field
2 mm = 2000 µm

soil particle
1 mm long or
1000 µm long

soil particle
$\frac{1}{2}$ mm long or
500 µm long

Figure 1.13 A soil particle under the microscope.

If the soil particle comes half way across the field of view it is 1000 µm long. There is a relationship between the power of an objective lens and its field of view. As the power of an objective lens increases the size of its field of view decreases.

◆ SUMMARY ◆

◆ A part of a body that performs a task to keep a living thing alive is called an organ (*see page 1*).

◆ There are ten organ systems in the human body. They are the sensory system, nervous system, respiratory system, digestive system, circulatory system, excretory system, skeletal system, muscle system, endocrine system and reproductive system (*see page 1*).

◆ There are four main organs in the body of a flowering plant. They are the root, stem, leaf and flower (*see page 3*).

◆ The bodies of plants and animals are made of cells. The basic parts of the cell are the nucleus, cytoplasm and cell membrane (*see page 6*).

◆ In a plant cell there is a cellulose cell wall and a vacuole (*see page 6*).

◆ Cells have different forms for different functions. They are adapted to perform specific tasks in the body and life of the organism (*see page 7*).

◆ The microscope is used to observe very small living things or the cells of larger living things (*see page 10*).

◆ There are special techniques for finding the size of a small object with the microscope (*see page 12*).

End of chapter question

1 If organisms as complex as us have developed on a planet similar to but with a stronger force of gravity than Earth, what body features would you expect them to have?

2 Food

Figure 2.1 Food for sale at a school canteen.

Some people do not eat breakfast. They have some sweets or crisps on the way to school. At break they eat a chocolate bar or have a fizzy drink. At lunch time they always have chips with their meal. In the afternoon they have some more sweets and for their evening meal they avoid green vegetables. Through the evening they have snacks of sweets, crisps and fizzy drinks.

Other people eat a breakfast of cereals and milk, toast and fruit juice. They eat an apple at break and have a range of lunch time meals through the week which include different vegetables, pasta and rice. In the afternoon they may have an orange and eat an evening meal with green vegetables. They may have a milky drink at bed time.

Nutrients

A chemical that is needed by the body to keep it in good health is called a nutrient. The human body needs a large number of different nutrients to keep it healthy. They can be divided up into the following nutrient groups:

- carbohydrates
- fats
- proteins
- vitamins
- minerals.

In addition to these nutrients the body also needs water. It accounts for 70% of the body's weight and provides support for the cells, it carries dissolved materials around the body and it helps in controlling body temperature.

1 Write a description of your daily eating pattern.

2 Compare your pattern with the two on this page. Which one does your pattern resemble?

3 From what you already know, try to explain which diet is more healthy.

For discussion

How healthy is your eating pattern? What changes would make it healthier? Do other people agree?

Carbohydrates

Carbohydrates are made from the elements carbon, hydrogen and oxygen. The atoms of these elements are linked together to form molecules of sugar. There are different types of sugar molecule but the most commonly occurring is glucose. Glucose molecules link together in long chains to make larger molecules, such as starch. Glucose and starch are two of the most widely known carbohydrates but there are others, such as cellulose.

in starch, each of these links is a glucose molecule

Figure 2.2 Carbohydrate molecule.

Fats

Fats are made of large numbers of carbon and hydrogen atoms linked together into long chains together with a few oxygen atoms. There are two kinds of fats – the solid fats produced by animals, such as lard, and the liquid fat or oil produced by plants, such as sunflower oil.

Proteins

Proteins are made from atoms of carbon, hydrogen, oxygen and nitrogen. Some proteins also contain sulphur and phosphorus. The atoms of these elements join together to make molecules of amino acids. Amino acids link together into long chains to form protein molecules.

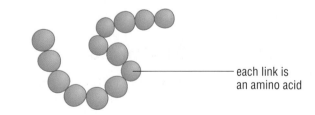

each link is an amino acid

Figure 2.3 Protein molecule.

4 What elements are found in carbohydrates, fats and proteins?

5 Which two words are used to describe the structure of carbohydrate, fat and protein molecules?

6 A science teacher held up a necklace of beads to her class and said it was a model of a protein molecule. What did each bead represent?

Vitamins

Unlike carbohydrates, fats and proteins, which are needed by the body in large amounts, vitamins are only needed in small amounts. When the vitamins were first discovered they were named after letters of the alphabet. Later, when the chemical structure of their molecules had been worked out, they were given chemical names.

Minerals

The body needs 20 different minerals to keep healthy. Some minerals, such as calcium, are needed in large amounts but others, such as zinc, are needed in only tiny amounts and are known as trace elements.

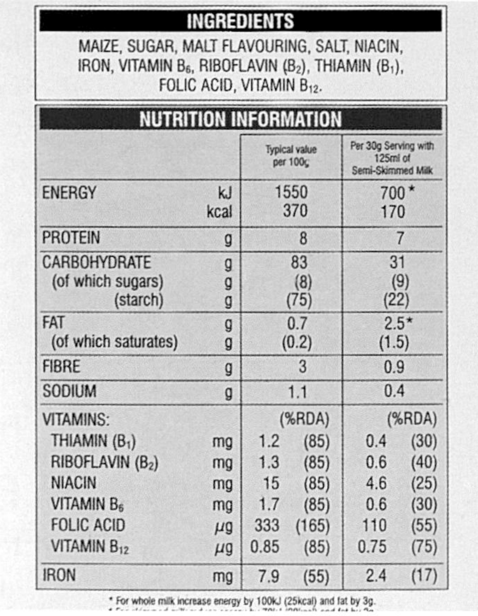

INGREDIENTS			
MAIZE, SUGAR, MALT FLAVOURING, SALT, NIACIN, IRON, VITAMIN B$_6$, RIBOFLAVIN (B$_2$), THIAMIN (B$_1$), FOLIC ACID, VITAMIN B$_{12}$.			

NUTRITION INFORMATION			
		Typical value per 100g	Per 30g Serving with 125ml of Semi-Skimmed Milk
ENERGY	kJ	1550	700 *
	kcal	370	170
PROTEIN	g	8	7
CARBOHYDRATE	g	83	31
(of which sugars)	g	(8)	(9)
(starch)	g	(75)	(22)
FAT	g	0.7	2.5*
(of which saturates)	g	(0.2)	(1.5)
FIBRE	g	3	0.9
SODIUM	g	1.1	0.4
VITAMINS:		(%RDA)	(%RDA)
THIAMIN (B$_1$)	mg	1.2 (85)	0.4 (30)
RIBOFLAVIN (B$_2$)	mg	1.3 (85)	0.6 (40)
NIACIN	mg	15 (85)	4.6 (25)
VITAMIN B$_6$	mg	1.7 (85)	0.6 (30)
FOLIC ACID	μg	333 (165)	110 (55)
VITAMIN B$_{12}$	μg	0.85 (85)	0.75 (75)
IRON	mg	7.9 (55)	2.4 (17)

* For whole milk increase energy by 100kJ (25kcal) and fat by 3g.

Figure 2.4 The nutrients in a food product are displayed on the side of the packet.

How the body uses nutrients

Carbohydrates

Carbohydrates contain a large amount of energy that can be released quickly inside the body. They are used as fuels to provide the energy for keeping the body alive. Cellulose, which makes up the walls of plant cells, is a carbohydrate. We cannot digest it but its presence in our food gives the food a solid property. This allows the muscles of the gut to push the food along, aiding digestion and preventing constipation. Cellulose in food is known as dietary fibre.

Fats

Fats are needed for the formation of cell membranes. They also contain even larger amounts of energy than carbohydrates. The body cannot release the energy in fats as quickly as the energy in carbohydrates so fats are used to store energy. In mammals the fat forms a layer under the skin. This acts as a heat insulator and helps to keep the mammal warm in cool conditions. Many mammals increase their body fat in the autumn so that they can draw on the stored energy if little food can be found in the winter. Some plants store oil in their seeds.

Proteins

Proteins are needed for building the structures in cells and in the formation of tissues and organs. They are needed for the growth of the body, to repair damaged parts, such as cut skin, and to replace tissues that are constantly being worn away, such as the lining of the mouth.

Chemicals that take part in the reactions for digesting food and in speeding up reactions inside cells are called enzymes. These are also made from proteins.

Vitamins

Each vitamin has one or more uses in the body. Vitamin A is involved in allowing the eyes to see in dim light and in making a mucus lining to the respiratory, digestive and excretory systems which protects against infection from microorganisms.

There are several B vitamins of which vitamin B_1 (thiamin) is an example (see the box, Finding the cause of beriberi, page 18).

A lack of vitamin C causes the deficiency disease called scurvy. As the disease develops bleeding occurs at the gums in the mouth, under the skin and into the joints. Death may occur due to massive bleeding in the body.

Vitamin D helps the body take up calcium from food to make strong bones and teeth. Children who have a lack of vitamin D in the diet develop the deficiency disease called rickets, in which the bones do not develop to their full strength and may therefore bend. This is seen particularly in the leg bones. Look at the X-ray in Figure 2.5.

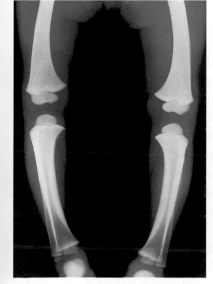

Figure 2.5 This child is suffering from rickets. It can be prevented by adding vitamin D to the diet.

Table 2.1 Vitamins and their uses.

Vitamin	Effect on body	Good sources
A	Increased resistance to disease Helps eyes to see in the dark	Milk, liver, cod-liver oil
B_1	Prevents digestive disorders Prevents the disease beriberi	Bread, milk
C	Prevents the disease scurvy in which gums bleed and the circulatory system is damaged	Blackcurrant, orange, lemon
D	Prevents the disease rickets in which bones become soft and leg bones of children may bend	Egg yolk, butter, cod-liver oil

Finding the cause of beriberi

Christiaan Eijkman (1858–1930) was a Dutch doctor who worked at a medical school in the East Indies in the late 19th Century. He investigated the disease called beriberi. In this disease the nerves fail to work properly and the action of the muscles becomes weak. All movements, especially walking, become difficult and as the disease progresses the heart may stop.

At this time other scientists had recently shown that microorganisms cause a number of diseases. It seemed reasonable to think that beriberi was also caused by a microorganism of some kind. Eijkman set up investigations to find it. He was not having any success. Then one day a flock of chickens that were kept at the medical school began to show the symptoms of beriberi.

Figure A   A flock of hens with beriberi.

1 What are the symptoms of beriberi?
2 How serious is the disease?
3 Why did Eijkman begin by looking for microorganisms as a cause of beriberi?
4 In what way did chance play a part in the discovery of the cause of beriberi? Explain your answer.
5 Write down a plan of an investigation to check Eijkman's work on chickens and beriberi. How would you make sure it was fair and that the results were reliable?
6 How did Eijkman's work alter the way scientists thought diseases developed?
7 What is the danger in having a diet which mainly features polished rice? Explain your answer.

Eijkman tested them for signs of the microorganisms that he believed were causing the disease. Again he had no success in linking the disease to the microorganisms but while he was studying the chickens, they recovered from the disease. Eijkman began to search for a reason why they had developed the disease and also why they had recovered so quickly. He discovered that the chickens were usually fed on chicken feed (a specially prepared mixture of foods that kept them healthy). A cook who had been working at the medical school had stopped using the chicken feed and had fed the chickens on rice that had been prepared for the patients. This cook had left and a new cook had been employed who would not let the rice be fed to the chickens. The birds were once again fed on the chicken feed. When Eijkman fed the chickens on rice again they developed beriberi. When he fed them on chicken feed they recovered from the disease straight away.

The rice fed to the chickens and the patients was polished rice. This had had its outer skin removed and appeared white. Later work by scientists showed that the skin of the rice contained vitamin B_1 or thiamin. This vitamin is needed to keep the nerves healthy and prevent beriberi.

For discussion

Eijkman performed his experiments on animals. Question 5 asked you to plan an investigation to check his work. Your plan may have featured studying animals. A great deal of information that benefits humans has been gathered by studying animals in experiments. Are there any guidelines that you would want scientists to follow in experiments involving animals?

7 A meal contains carbohydrate, fat, protein, vitamin D, calcium and iron. What is the fate of each of these substances in the body?

8 Which carbohydrate cannot be digested by humans and how does it help the digestive system?

9 In a patient suffering from rickets why do the leg bones bend more than the arm bones?

10 A seal is a mammal. How can it survive in the cold polar seas when a human would die in a few minutes?

Figure 2.6 Seals on the ice.

Minerals

Each mineral may have more than one use. For example, calcium is needed to make strong bones and teeth. It is also used to make muscles work and for blood to clot. A lack of calcium in the diet can lead to weak bones and high blood pressure. The mineral iron is used to make the red blood pigment called haemoglobin.

Water

About 70% of the human body is water. The body can survive for only a few days without a drink of water.

Every chemical reaction in the body takes place in water. The blood is made mainly from water. It is the liquid that transports all the other blood components around the body.

Water is used to cool down the body by evaporation of sweat from the skin.

The amounts of nutrients in food

The amounts of nutrients in foods have been worked out by experiment and calculation. The amounts are usually expressed for a sample of food weighing 100 g. Table 2.2 shows the nutrients in a small range of common foods.

Table 2.2 The nutrients in some common foods.

Food (100 g)	Protein (g)	Fat (g)	Carbohydrate (g)	Calcium (mg)	Iron (mg)	Vit C (mg)	Vit D (µg)
Potato	2.1	0	18.0	8	0.7	8–30	0
Carrot	0.7	0	5.4	48	0.6	.6	0
Bread	9.6	3.1	46.7	28	3.0	0	0
Spaghetti	9.9	1.0	84.0	23	1.2	0	0
Rice	6.2	1.0	86.8	4	0.4	0	0
Lentil	23.8	0	53.2	39	7.6	0	0
Pea	5.8	0	10.6	15	1.9	25	0
Jam	0.5	0	69.2	18	1.2	10	0
Peanut	28.1	49.0	8.6	61	2.0	0	0
Lamb	15.9	30.2	0	7	1.3	0	0
Milk	3.3	3.8	4.8	120	0.1	1	0.05
Cheese 1	25.4	35.4	0	810	0.6	0	0.35
Cheese 2	15.3	4.0	4.5	80	0.4	0	0.02
Butter	0.5	81.0	0	15	0.2	0	1.25
Chicken	20.8	6.7	0	11	1.5	0	0
Egg	12.3	10.9	0	54	2.1	0	1.50
Fish 1	17.4	0.7	0	16	0.3	0	0
Fish 2	16.8	18.5	0	33	0.8	0	22.20
Apple	0.3	0	12.0	4	0.3	5	0
Banana	1.1	0	19.2	7	0.4	10	0
Orange	0.8	0	8.5	41	0.3	50	0

Notes for Tables 2.2 and 2.3
Vegetables are raw; the bread is wholemeal bread; cheese 1 is cheddar cheese; cheese 2 is cottage cheese; fish 1 is a white fish, such as cod; fish 2 is an oily fish, such as herring.

11 In Table 2.2, which foods
    contain the most
    a) protein, **b)** fat,
    c) carbohydrate, **d)** calcium,
    e) iron, **f)** vitamin C and
    g) vitamin D?

12 Which foods would a
    vegetarian not eat?

13 Which foods would a
    vegetarian have to eat more of
    and why?

14 Which food provides all the
    nutrients?

15 Why might you expect this
    food to contain so many
    nutrients?

Keeping a balance

In order to remain healthy the diet has to be balanced
with the body's needs. A balanced diet is one in which
all the nutrients are present in the correct amounts to
keep the body healthy. You do not need to know the
exact amounts of nutrients in each food to work out
whether you have a healthy diet. A simple way is to look
at a chart showing food divided into groups, with the
main nutrients of each group displayed (see Table 2.4).
You can then see if you eat at least one portion from
each group each day and more portions of the food
groups that lack fat. Remember that you also need to
include fibre even though it is not digested. It is essential
for the efficient working of the muscles in the alimentary
canal. Fibre is found in cereals, vegetables and pulses,
such as peas and beans.

16 Table 2.3 shows the amount of
    energy provided by 100 g of
    each of the foods shown in
    Table 2.2. Arrange the nine
    highest energy foods in order
    starting with the highest and
    ending with the lowest. Look at
    the nutrient content of these
    foods in Table 2.2.
    a) Do you think the energy is
    stored as fat or as
    carbohydrate in each of the
    nine highest energy foods?
    b) Arrange the foods into
    groups according to where
    you think the energy is
    stored.
    c) Do the food stores you have
    identified store the same
    amount of energy (see also
    page 16)? Explain your
    answer.

17 Why might people who are
    trying to lose weight eat
    cottage cheese instead of
    cheddar cheese?

18 Mackerel is an oily fish.
    Describe the nutrients you
    would expect it to contain.

Table 2.3 The energy value of some common foods.

Food (100 g)	Energy (kJ)
Potato	324
Carrot	98
Bread	1025
Spaghetti	1549
Rice	1531
Lentil	1256
Pea	273
Jam	1116
Peanut	2428
Lamb	1388
Milk	274
Cheese 1	1708
Cheese 2	480
Butter	3006
Chicken	602
Egg	612
Fish 1	321
Fish 2	970
Apple	197
Banana	326
Orange	150

19 Look again at the eating pattern you prepared for Question 1 on page 14. Analyse your diet into the food groups shown in Table 2.4. How well does your diet provide you with all the nutrients you need?

Table 2.4 The groups of foods and their nutrients.

Vegetables and fruit	Cereals	Pulses	Meat and eggs	Milk products
Carbohydrates	Carbohydrates	Carbohydrates	Protein	Protein
Vitamin A	Protein	Protein	Fat	Fat
Vitamin C	B vitamins	B vitamins	B vitamins	Vitamin A
Minerals	Minerals	Iron	Iron	B vitamins
Fibre	Fibre	Fibre		Vitamin C
				Calcium

20 Table 2.5 shows how the energy requirements of an average male and female person change from the age of 2 to 25 years. Plot graphs of the information given in the table.

21 Describe what the graphs show.

22 Explain why there is a difference in energy needs between a 2-year-old child and an 8-year-old child.

23 Explain why there is a difference in energy needs between an 18-year-old male and an 18-year-old female.

24 Explain why there is a change in the energy needs as a person ages from 18 to 25.

25 What changes would you expect in the energy used by:
a) a 25-year-old person who changed from a job delivering mail to working with a computer
b) a 25-year-old person who gave up working with computers and took a job on a building site that involved carrying heavy loads
c) a 25-year-old female during pregnancy?

Table 2.5 Average daily energy used by males and females.

| Age (years) | Daily energy used (kJ) | |
	Male	Female
2	5500	5500
5	7000	7000
8	8800	8800
11	10 000	9200
14	12 500	10 500
18	14 200	9600
25	12 100	8800

Malnutrition

If the diet provides too few nutrients or too many nutrients malnutrition occurs. Lack of a nutrient in a diet may produce a deficiency disease, such as scurvy or anaemia. Scurvy is a deficiency disease caused by a lack of vitamin C and anaemia is a deficiency disease caused by a lack of iron.

If more protein than is needed is eaten, it is broken down in the body. Part of it is converted to a carbohydrate called glycogen, which is stored in the liver, and part of it is converted to a chemical called urea, which is excreted in the urine.

Too much high energy food such as carbohydrate and fat leads to the body becoming overweight. If the body is extremely overweight it is described as obese. If too little high energy food is eaten the body becomes thin

26 What happens in the body if too much fat, carbohydrate or protein is eaten?

27 Why do people become thin if they do not eat enough high energy food?

because it uses up energy stored as fat. Energy stored in protein in the muscles can also be used up.

The condition anorexia nervosa can lead to extreme weight loss and possibly death. It occurs mainly in teenage girls but can also occur in teenage boys. People suffering from anorexia nervosa eat very little and may fear becoming overweight. As soon as the condition is diagnosed, they need careful counselling to stand the best chance of making a full recovery.

A healthy diet

The body needs a range of nutrients to keep healthy (see pages 14–19) and everyone should eat a balanced diet (see page 21) to provide these nutrients. Regular eating of high energy snacks, such as sweets, chocolate, crisps, ice-cream and chips, between meals unbalances the diet and can lead to the body becoming overweight, damage to the teeth (see page 64) and ill-health. Overweight people have to make more effort than normal to move so they tend to take less exercise. In time this can affect the heart (see page 57).

High energy snacks should be kept to a minimum so that the main meals of the day, which provide most of the essential nutrients, may be eaten. There are alternatives to high energy snacks. These are fruits and raw vegetables, such as celery, tomatoes and carrots. In addition to being lower in energy they also provide more vitamins and minerals.

◆ SUMMARY ◆

- ◆ A chemical that is needed by the body to keep it healthy is called a nutrient (*see page 14*).
- ◆ The groups of nutrients are carbohydrates, fats, proteins, vitamins and minerals (*see page 15*).
- ◆ Each nutrient has a specific use in the body (*see page 16*).
- ◆ Different foods have different amounts of nutrients (*see page 20*).
- ◆ A balanced diet needs to be eaten for good health (*see page 21*).
- ◆ Water and fibre are essential components of the diet (*see pages 19 and 21*).

End of chapter questions

1 What is a healthy diet?

2 Do animals prefer certain foods? A pair of zebra finches were tested with a seed mixture bought from a pet shop to see if they preferred to eat certain seeds in the mixture. A sample of the mixture was left in a dish in the birds' cage for 6 hours. At the end of that time the sample was removed and the seeds were separated into their different types. A sample of the original mixture, called the bulk, that was similar in size to the dish sample was also sorted into the different seed types.

Table 2.6

	Type A Millet	Type B Round brown seeds	Type C Elongate grey seeds	Type D Small round seeds	Type E Black seeds
Dish (total sample = 218)	25	39	27	124	3
Bulk (total sample = 288)	120	27	41	97	3

Table 2.6 shows the composition of the two samples. Table 2.7 shows the percentage of each type of seed in the two samples.

Table 2.7

	Type A	Type B	Type C	Type D	Type E
Dish	12	14	13	59	1.5
Bulk	42	9	14	34	1
Difference (D–B)	−30	+5	−1	+25	–

a) Why was the dish sample left for 6 hours in the bird cage?

b) How was the test made fair?

c) Why could the figures for the seeds in the two samples in Table 2.6 not be compared directly?

d) How is the percentage of the seed type worked out?

e) Check the percentage of millet in both samples. How have the figures been processed?

f) If the dish sample had roughly the same composition as the bulk sample when it was first put in the birds' cage, **i)** which seeds have the birds eaten and **ii)** which have they most strongly avoided?

g) How could you find out more about the birds' food preferences?

3 | *Digestion*

Your food comes from the tissues of animals and plants. To enter the cells of your body the tissues have to be broken down. This releases the nutrients (carbohydrates, proteins, fats, minerals and vitamins). Some of them are in the form of long chain molecules. They must be broken down into smaller molecules that dissolve in water and can pass through the wall of the gut. This process of making the food into a form that can be taken into the body is called digestion. It takes place in the digestive system, which is made up of the alimentary canal and organs such as the liver and pancreas.

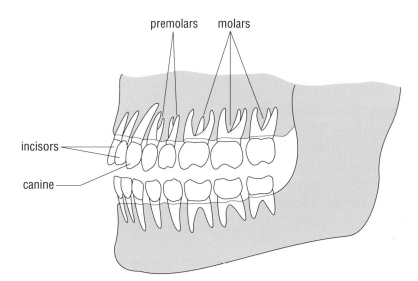

Figure 3.1 The four types of teeth in the mouth.

Teeth

When food enters your mouth the first structures it meets are your teeth. There are four kinds of teeth. The chisel-shaped incisor teeth are at the front of the mouth. These are for biting into soft foods like fruits. Next to the incisors are the canines. These are pointed and in dogs and cats form the fang teeth that are used for tearing into tougher food like meat. Humans do not eat much tough food so they use their canines as extra incisors. The premolars and the molars are similar in appearance. They have raised parts called cusps with grooves between them. They form a crushing and grinding surface at the back of the mouth. The action of the teeth breaks up the food into small pieces.

The first teeth form in the gums of the embryo 6 weeks after fertilisation but they do not break through the gums until about 6 months after the baby is born. The incisors emerge first followed by the first molars when the baby is 12 months old. At 18 months the canines emerge and by 3 years of age the child has a full set of 20 milk teeth.

As the child grows the jaw gets larger and the milk teeth are too small to fill the gums. Their roots are absorbed by the body and their crowns become loose and eventually fall out. The milk teeth are replaced by a set of permanent teeth. With care, these can last a lifetime.

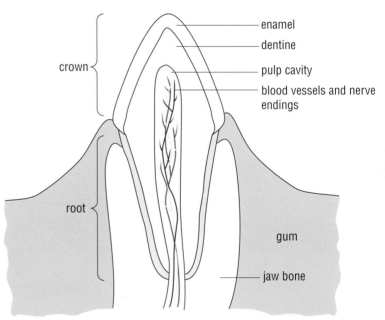

Figure 3.2 The parts of a tooth.

1 Figure 3.1 shows the arrangement of the permanent teeth in half of the mouth. How many teeth make up a complete set of permanent teeth? How many incisor, canine, premolar and molar teeth are there?

2 How are the molars in the upper jaw different from those in the lower jaw? Explain the difference.

3 What teeth would you expect to see in the mouth of an 18-month-old child?

4 When a set of milk teeth is replaced by a set of permanent teeth, how many more teeth are there in the mouth?

5 What do you think the nerve endings in the teeth are sensitive to?

6 How might the teeth of a meat-eating animal, such as a lion, be different from the teeth of a plant-eating animal, such as a zebra?

7 What is the purpose of the teeth?

The part of the tooth you see above your gums is the crown. Below the crown is the root which holds the tooth in the jaw bone. The white substance covering the surface of the tooth is a layer of enamel. It is the hardest substance in the body but it is also brittle. Beneath the enamel is the dentine. This forms the bulk of the tooth. It is hard like enamel but not brittle. It has strands of living tissue running through it. The strands spread out from the pulp cavity at the centre of the tooth. This space contains living tissues, tiny blood vessels called capillaries and nerve endings. The blood brings food and oxygen to the living cells in the pulp cavity and takes away their waste. The root is held in place by cement and fibres of protein.

Early ideas about digestion

At one time there were two ideas about how food was digested. Some scientists believed that the stomach churned up the food to break it up physically and others believed that a chemical process took place.

Andreas Vesalius (1514–1564) was a Flemish doctor who investigated the structure of the human body by dissection. He had an artist make drawings of his work and these were published in a book for others to study.

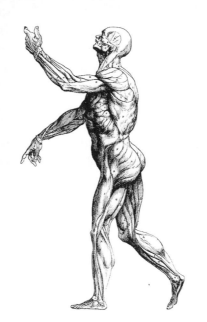

Figure A   A drawing of Vesalius's work.

1 How was Vesalius's work recorded?
2 How life-like were the recordings of Vesalius's work?
3 How did the idea that the stomach acted as a churning machine develop?
4 If Borelli's idea had been correct what would Réaumur have found?
5 What did Réaumur's investigation show?
6 Do you think Réaumur's investigation threatened the hawk's life? Explain your answer.

René Descartes (1596–1650) studied mathematics and astronomy. He believed that all actions were due to mechanical movements. When he saw the drawings of Vesalius's dissections he believed that the human body behaved just as a machine.

Giovanni Borelli (1608–1679) studied the parts of the body and Descartes's ideas. He showed how muscles pulled on bones to make them move and how the bones acted as levers. This work supported Descartes's ideas, and Borelli extended it to consider the stomach as a churning machine for breaking up food.

Franciscus Sylvius (1614–1672), a German doctor, believed that chemical processes took place in the body and that digestion was a chemical process that began in the mouth with the action of saliva. Some other scientists believed in his ideas.

Figure B   A hawk eating a meal.

In 1752 René Réaumur (1683–1757), a French scientist, decided to test these two ideas by studying the digestion in a hawk. When a hawk feeds it swallows large pieces of its prey, digests the meat and regurgitates fur, feathers and bones that it cannot digest. Réaumur put some meat inside small metal cylinders and covered the ends with a metal gauze. He fed the cylinders to the hawk and waited for the hawk to regurgitate them. He found that some of the meat had dissolved but the cylinders and gauze showed no signs of being ground up as if by a machine. To follow up his experiment he fed a sponge to the hawk to collect some of the stomach juices. When the hawk regurgitated the sponge Réaumur squeezed out the stomach juices and poured them on to a sample of meat. Slowly the meat dissolved.

Chemical breakdown of food

Proteins, fats and carbohydrates are made from large molecules which are made from smaller molecules that are linked together. The large molecules do not dissolve in water and cannot pass through the lining of the digestive system into the body. The smaller molecules from which they are made, however, *do* dissolve in water and *do* pass through the wall of the digestive system. Almost all reactions in living things involve chemicals called enzymes. They are made by the body from proteins and they speed up chemical reactions. Digestive enzymes speed up the breakdown of the large molecules into smaller ones.

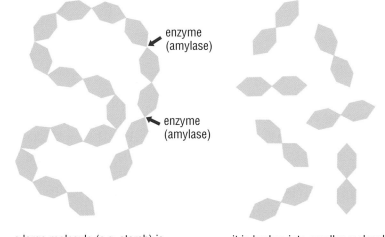

enzyme (amylase)

enzyme (amylase)

8 Which smaller molecules join together to form
a) carbohydrates and
b) protein (see also page 15)?
9 What do enzymes in the digestive system do?

a large molecule (e.g. starch) is attacked by an enzyme

it is broken into smaller molecules (e.g. the sugar maltose)

Figure 3.3   The action of an enzyme on a large food molecule.

Along the alimentary canal

When your mouth waters

The 'water' that occurs in your mouth is called saliva. You can make up to $1\frac{1}{2}$ litres of saliva in 24 hours. Saliva is made by three pairs of salivary glands. The glands are made up of groups of cells that produce the saliva, and ducts (tubes) that deliver it to the mouth.

Saliva is 99% water but it also contains a slimy substance called mucin and an enzyme called amylase which begins the digestion of starch in the food. The mucin coats the food and makes it easier to swallow. Amylase begins the breakdown of starch molecules into sugar molecules.

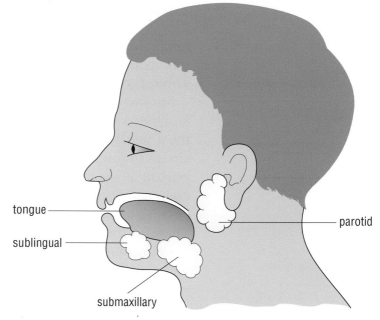

Figure 3.4 The salivary glands.

When you swallow

When you have chewed your food it is made into a pellet called the bolus. This is pushed to the back of your mouth by your tongue. Swallowing causes the bolus to slide down your gullet, which is the tube connecting the mouth to the stomach. This tube is also called the oesophagus. It has two layers of muscles in its walls.

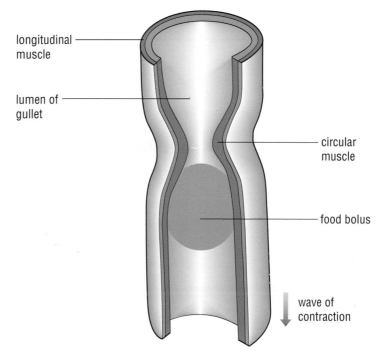

Figure 3.5 The structure of the gullet and the process of peristalsis.

In the outer layer the muscle cells are arranged so that they point along the length of the gullet. These form the longitudinal muscle layer. In the inner layer the cells are arranged so that they point around the wall of the gullet. These form the circular muscle layer.

Muscle cells can contract or get shorter. They cannot lengthen on their own, so another set of muscle cells must work to lengthen them. In the gullet, when the circular muscles contract, they squeeze on the food and push it along the tube. The longitudinal muscles then contract to stretch the circular muscles once again. The circular muscles do not all contract at the same time. Those at the top of the gullet contract first then a region lower down follows and so on until the food is pushed into the stomach. This wave of muscular contraction is called peristalsis. Peristaltic waves also occur in other parts of the alimentary canal to push the food along.

Stomach

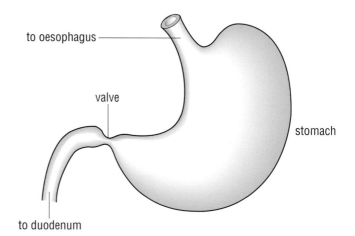

to oesophagus

valve

stomach

to duodenum

Figure 3.6 The stomach.

The stomach wall is lined with glands. These produce hydrochloric acid and a protein-digesting enzyme called pepsin. The hydrochloric acid kills many kinds of bacteria in the food and provides the acid conditions that pepsin needs to start breaking down protein in the food.

The food is churned up by the action of the muscles as they send peristaltic waves down the stomach walls at the rate of about three per minute. The food is prevented from leaving the stomach by a valve. When the food is broken down into a creamy liquid the valve opens which allows the liquid food to pass through into the next part of the digestive system.

A hole in the stomach

In 1822 a group of fur trappers and hunters gathered at a trading post, Fort Mackinac, USA. One of the hunters accidentally fired his gun and shot a 19-year-old man called Alexis St Martin. It was fortunate that Doctor William Beaumont (1785–1853) was close by and could attend to the wounded man and save his life. St Martin had lost some flesh from over his stomach and part of the stomach wall. The wound did not completely heal. It formed a flap over the stomach which could be opened and the contents of the stomach examined.

St Martin agreed to help Beaumont to find out what happened inside the stomach during digestion. First Beaumont asked St Martin to eat nothing for a few hours then he looked inside the stomach and found that the stomach contained saliva, which St Martin had swallowed, and some mucus from the stomach wall.

In another experiment Beaumont put some bread crumbs into the stomach and saw digestive juice start to collect on the wall of the stomach.

Beaumont wanted to find out what happened to food in the stomach. So, he fastened pieces of cooked and raw meat, bread and cabbage onto silk strings and pushed them through the hole. An hour later he pulled the strings out and found that about half the cabbage and bread had broken up but the meat remained the same. Another hour later he found that the cooked meat had started to break down.

Next Beaumont wanted to find out what happened to the food after St Martin had eaten it. He gave St Martin a meal of fish, potatoes, bread and parsnips. After half an hour Beaumont examined the stomach contents and found that he could still identify pieces of fish and potato. After another half hour pieces of potato could still be seen but most of the fish had broken up. One and a half hours after the meal all the pieces of the food had broken up. Two hours after the meal the stomach was empty.

1 In the first experiment Beaumont was interested to find out if the stomach contained digestive juices all the time, even when no food was present.
   a) What conclusion could he draw from his observation?
   b) What prediction could he make from this observation?
2 What do you think Beaumont concluded from his second experiment?
3 The juices contain important chemicals made by the body. What are these called?
4 What did you think Beaumont concluded from his experiments with food on strings?
5 What do you think Beaumont concluded from his experiment on St Martin's meal?
6 Beaumont also investigated the action of the stomach juice outside the stomach. Why would he have kept the juice at body temperature?
7 If you were Alexis St Martin would you have allowed Dr Beaumont to carry out his investigation? Explain your reasons.

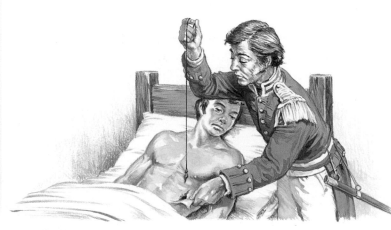

Figure A   Doctor Beaumont placing a piece of food into Alexis St Martin's stomach.

Duodenum, liver and pancreas

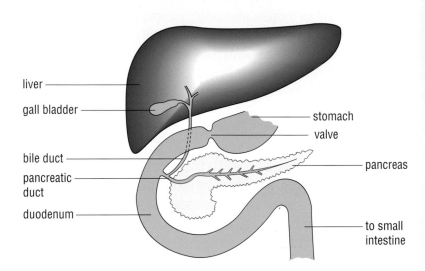

Figure 3.7   The duodenum, liver and pancreas.

The duodenum is a tube that connects the stomach to the small intestine. Two other tubes are connected to it. One tube carries a green liquid called bile from the gall bladder to mix with the food. Bile is made in the liver and contains chemicals that help break down fat into small droplets so that fat-digesting enzymes can work more easily. The second tube comes from an organ called the pancreas. This is a gland that produces a juice containing enzymes that digest proteins, fats and carbohydrates. The mixture of liquids from the stomach, liver and pancreas pass on into the small intestine.

Small intestine

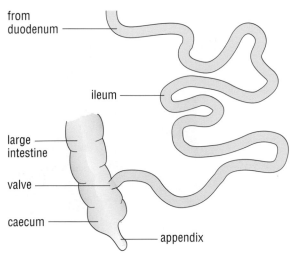

Figure 3.8   The small intestine.

10 How does saliva help in digesting food?

11 What is peristalsis?

12 What does hydrochloric acid do?

13 Where is bile made and what does it do?

14 What are proteins, fats and carbohydrates broken down into?

15 Where are the digested foods absorbed?

The cells lining the wall of the small intestine make enzymes that complete the digestion of carbohydrates and proteins. Proteins are broken down into amino acids, carbohydrates are broken down into sugars, and fats are broken down into fatty acids and glycerol. All these small molecules are soluble and can pass through the wall of the small intestine. They are carried by the blood to all cells of the body.

Fate of undigested food

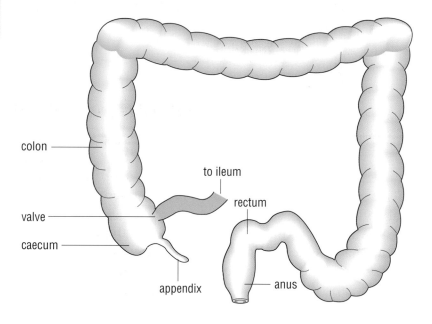

Figure 3.9 The large intestine and rectum.

Indigestible parts of the food, such as cellulose, pass on through the small intestine to the large intestine and colon. Here water and some dissolved vitamins are absorbed and taken into the body. The remaining semi-solid substances form the faeces which are stored in the rectum. The faeces are removed from the body through the anus perhaps once or twice a day in a process called egestion.

16 What happens to undigested food in the large intestine?

17 What happens in egestion?

Enzymes

An enzyme that digests carbohydrate is called a carbohydrase. An enzyme that digests protein is called a protease. An enzyme that digests fat is called a lipase.

18 What kind of enzyme is produced in **a)** the mouth and **b)** the stomach?

19 What kind of enzyme does bile help?

20 Where does bile come from?

21 Which organ of the digestive system produces all three kinds of enzyme?

22 Why do small droplets of fat get broken down by enzymes more quickly than large droplets?

Table 3.1 Enzymes.

Region of production	Kind of enzyme	Notes
Salivary glands in mouth	Carbohydrase	Enzyme is called salivary amylase
Gastric glands in stomach	Protease	Enzyme is called pepsin Hydrochloric acid is also made to help the enzyme work
Pancreas	Protease, carbohydrase, lipase	Enzymes enter the duodenum and mix with food and bile

◆ SUMMARY ◆

♦ The purpose of digestion is to break down the food into substances that can be absorbed and used by the body (*see page 25*).

♦ There are four kinds of teeth. They are the incisors, canines, premolars and molars. They have special shapes for specific tasks (*see page 25*).

♦ Enzymes break down the large molecules in food into smaller molecules so that they can be absorbed by the body (*see page 28*).

♦ The food is moved along the gut by a wave of muscular contraction called peristalsis (*see page 29*).

♦ The food is digested by enzymes that are made in the salivary glands, the stomach wall, the pancreas and the wall of the small intestine (*see pages 28, 30, 32–33*).

♦ The liver produces bile which helps in the digestion of fat (*see page 32*).

♦ Digested food is absorbed in the small intestine (*see page 33*).

♦ The undigested food has water removed from it in the large intestine and is then stored in the rectum before being released through the anus (*see page 33*).

End of chapter questions

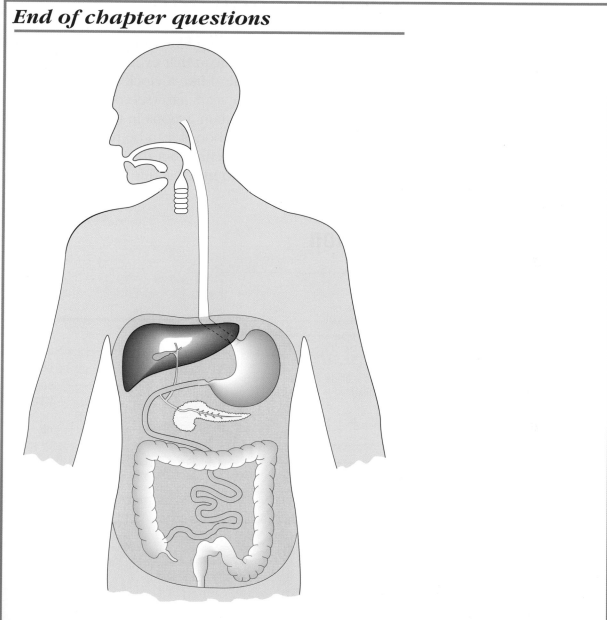

Figure 3.10

1 Collect a copy of Figure 3.10 from your teacher and use the other
   diagrams in this chapter to label all the parts of the digestive system.
2 Describe the digestion of a chicken sandwich.

4 | *The body machine*

The idea of the body working like a machine is a useful one. It does not have to mean that everything that takes place inside it is mechanical like a clockwork toy. This idea was tested over 200 years ago (see page 27) and found to be incorrect. Certain actions in the body, like the actions of muscles on bones, can be reproduced with springs and levers in a machine but the release of energy to give the body power to move is due to chemical reactions.

Skeleton

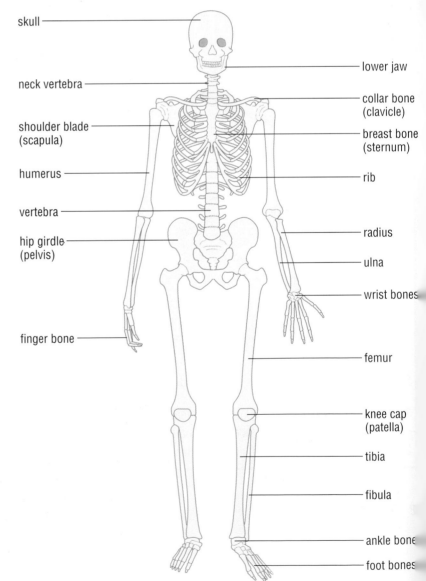

Figure 4.1 The skeleton.

1 There are three bones in the arm. How many are in the wrist and hand?
2 How many bones are in all four limbs?
3 A person has a mass of 43.5 kg. What is the mass of their skeleton?
4 Figure 4.1 shows the main bones of the body. How many of these bones can you feel in your body?

There are 206 bones in the human skeleton. Each arm and hand together have 30 bones. Each leg and foot together have 29 bones. The skeleton accounts for 15% of the mass of the body. The tissue of the skeleton (bone) is hardened as it takes up calcium from the digested food.

The skeleton and protection

The brain and the spinal cord form the central nervous system and are made from soft tissue. They could be easily damaged without a hard covering. The bones of the skull are fused together to make a strong case around the brain. The backbone is made up of 33 bones known as vertebrae (*singular*: vertebra). There is a hole in each vertebra through which the spinal cord runs. The column of vertebrae make a tube of bone around the spinal cord. There are gaps between the vertebrae through which nerves pass from the spinal cord to the body. The ribs and backbone form a protective structure around the lungs and the heart.

5 The skull forms a solid sheet of protection and the ribs form a cage. Why do you think the rib cage is not a solid sheet like the skull? Which offers the better protection, the sheet or the cage? Explain your answer.

6 Newborn mammals have soft skeletons to allow some flexibility during birth. All mammals are fed milk by their mothers. What effect will this have on their bones?

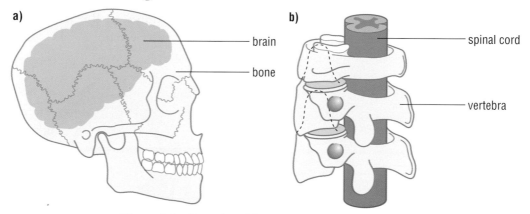

a) brain
bone

b) spinal cord
vertebra

Figure 4.2   Protection of the central nervous system, **a)** the brain and **b)** the spinal cord.

The skeleton and support

The organs that form systems such as digestive, circulatory, excretory and respiratory systems account for 20% of the body's weight. The organs are made from soft material and have no strong supporting material inside them. The bones of the skeleton provide a strong structure to which the organs are attached. They allow the organs to be spread out in the body without squashing into each other.

The muscles account for 45% of the body's weight. They are also made from soft tissue but gain their support from the bones to which they are attached.

7 A person has a mass of 43.5 kg. How much of this mass is due to
a) their organ systems and
b) their muscles?

8 The percentage of the body's mass not accounted for by the skeleton, organs and muscles is due to fat. What percentage of the body's mass is due to fat?

9   Look at the skeleton in Figure 4.1. Which bones meet at **a)** the hip joint, **b)** the knee joint, **c)** the elbow joint and **d)** the shoulder joint?
10 Name two **a)** hinge joints and **b)** ball and socket joints.
11 How might a joint be affected by **a)** torn ligaments, **b)** lack of synovial fluid and **c)** damaged cartilage?

The skeleton and movement

The place where bones meet is called a joint. In some joints, such as those in the skull, the bones are fused together and cannot move. Most joints, however, allow some movement. Some joints, such as the elbow or knee, are called hinge joints because the movement is like the hinge on a door. The bones can only move forwards or backwards. A few joints, such as the hip, are called ball and socket joints because the end of one bone forms a round structure like a ball which fits into a cup-shaped socket. These joints allow much more movement.

To stop the bones coming apart when they move, they are held together by tough fibres called ligaments. To stop them wearing out as they rub over each other, the parts of the bones in the joint are covered with cartilage. This substance has a hard, slippery surface that reduces friction and allows the bones to move over each other easily. In some joints, where there is a lot of movement, cells in a tissue called the synovial membrane make a liquid called synovial fluid. This fluid spreads out over the surfaces of the cartilage in the joint and acts like an oil, reducing friction and wear.

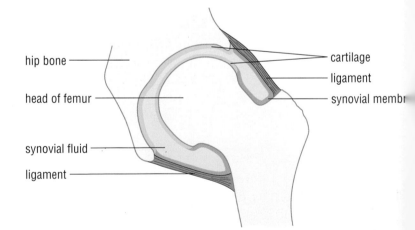

Labels: hip bone, head of femur, synovial fluid, ligament, cartilage, ligament, synovial membr[ane]

Figure 4.3   Inside a hip joint.

12 Why do you think that some joints are painful in elderly people?
13 How does the body stop you using a damaged joint so that it has time to heal?

For discussion

What would the body be like without a skeleton?

Could the body survive without a skeleton?

Muscles

Muscle is made up from tissue that has the power to move. It can contract to become shorter. A muscle is attached to two bones across a joint. When muscle gets shorter it exerts a pulling force. This moves one of the bones but the other stays stationary. For example, in the upper arm the biceps muscle is attached to the shoulder blade and to the radius bone in the forearm.

When the biceps shortens or contracts it exerts a pulling force on the radius and raises the forearm.

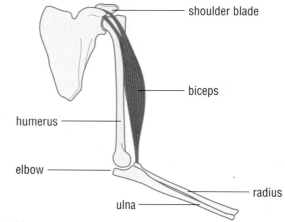

shoulder blade

biceps

humerus

elbow

radius

ulna

Figure 4.4 Biceps on arm bones.

A muscle cannot lengthen or extend itself. It needs a pulling force to stretch it again. This force is provided by another muscle. The two muscles are arranged so that when one contracts it pulls on the other muscle, which relaxes and lengthens. For example, in the upper arm the triceps muscle is attached to the shoulder blade, humerus and ulna. When it contracts, the biceps relaxes and the force exerted by the triceps lengthens the biceps and pulls the forearm down. When the biceps contracts again, the triceps relaxes and the force exerted by the biceps lengthens the triceps again and raises the forearm. The action of one muscle produces an opposite effect to the other muscle and causes movement in the opposite direction. The two muscles are therefore called an antagonistic muscle pair.

14 Draw a diagram featuring both the biceps and the triceps, showing the triceps fully shortened.

15 Using dotted lines, draw the position of the forearm when the biceps is fully shortened.

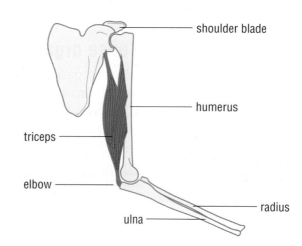

shoulder blade

humerus

triceps

elbow

radius

ulna

Figure 4.5 Triceps on arm bones.

Nervous control

The action of the muscles is co-ordinated by the nervous system. There are two parts to the nervous system. They are the central nervous system, which comprises the brain and spinal cord, and the peripheral nervous system, which is formed from the nerves connecting the sense organs, muscles and glands to the central nervous system.

Nerves are made from nerve cells or neurones which have long thread-like extensions. These nerve cells are connected to other nerve cells in the spinal cord. The nerve cells in the spinal cord are then connected to nerve cells in the brain.

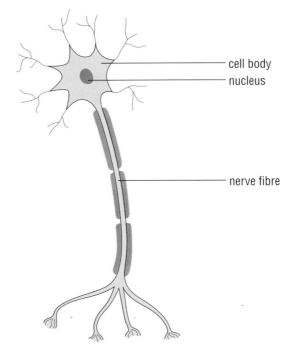

cell body
nucleus

nerve fibre

Figure 4.6 Nerve cell.

Sense organs and stimuli

Sense organs have nerve cells that can detect changes in the environment. These sensory cells send electrical signals to the central nervous system. Something in the environment that causes a sensory cell to send a signal is called a stimulus. The sound of a bell or a flash of light are just two examples of stimuli that can be detected by the body's sense organs. When the central nervous system receives a signal about a stimulus, it may send signals to other parts of the body to make them respond to the stimulus.

Responding to a stimulus

The simplest response to a stimulus is called a reflex response. The signal from the sense organ passes along three neurones from the sense organ to the muscle, to make the muscle contract. The arrangement of the sense organ, neurones and muscle that brings about a reflex response is called a reflex arc (see Figure 4.7). A reflex arc does not involve the brain and so the reaction is much faster.

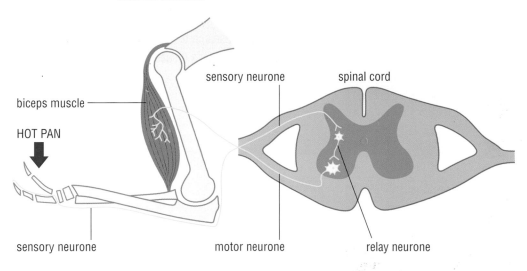

Figure 4.7 Reflex arc.

If you touch something very hot, such as a hot pan, you may move your hand away quickly. In this reflex response, heat receptors in your skin send signals along a sensory neurone. The signals pass to a relay neurone which then transfers them to a motor neurone. The signals travel along the motor neurone to the muscle. When they reach the muscle they make it contract. This contraction pulls the hand away from the hot object.

When the signal reaches the relay neurone in the spinal cord, it also travels along nerve cells up the spinal cord to the brain. This is not part of the reflex arc and does not produce reflex actions. The signal may pass to various parts of the brain and as a result of this, the brain may send out more signals to other parts of the body. For example, the brain may send signals to the voice box and chest so that the person releases a scream. If a valuable object has been picked up and the memory part of the brain has recorded this, signals may be sent to the muscles in the hand to put the object down safely and not to drop it.

For discussion

A football commentator described the quick action of a goalkeeper to tip the ball over the cross bar as a reflex action? Is this correct? Explain your answer.

Nerve growth

Rita Levi-Montalcini (1909–) studied how nerves grew and worked. She learnt how to grow nerves in the laboratory so that they could be studied separately from other kinds of cells. From her work, Levi-Montalcini discovered a substance that stimulated nerves to grow. She called this substance nerve growth factor (NGF) and found that it helped the growth of all kinds of nerves. She began working with Stanley Cohen (1922–) and they discovered that NGF was found in an unlikely source – male mouse saliva. They also discovered that NGF was a protein and that antibodies could be made to stop its action. Levi-Montalcini and Cohen shared the 1986 Nobel Prize for physiology and medicine for their work. Their research has led to a greater understanding of nervous disorders such as Alzheimer's disease.

1 Why do you think male mouse saliva is an unlikely source of NGF?
2 If two nerves having NGF were being studied, how could antibodies be used to investigate the effect of NGF?

Figure A   Rita Levi-Montalcini.

Respiration

All life processes, not just movement, need energy. The energy is stored in food molecules. In the human body a sugar called glucose is the main source of energy. Most of it is formed by the digestion of starch. It dissolves in the blood and is transported to the cells.

Aerobic respiration

16 In the burning process, a fuel takes part in a chemical reaction with oxygen and produces the same products as in respiration. How is burning different from respiration?
17 What would happen if burning and respiration were identical?

Glucose takes part in a chemical reaction with oxygen inside the cell. During this reaction glucose is broken down to carbon dioxide and water, and energy is released. This process is called aerobic respiration. The reaction can be written as a word equation:

glucose + oxygen → carbon dioxide + water + energy

The energy is released slowly in a series of stages during respiration.

18 Put one arm straight up in the air. Clench and unclench your fist as fast as you can for as long as you can. What happens and why? Put your arm down. What happens now and why?

Anaerobic respiration

Muscle cells sometimes need oxygen faster than it can be supplied. This might happen when you sprint for the finishing tape in a race. The muscle cells still respire, but they use another method. They respire anaerobically – without oxygen. In this process the glucose is broken down to lactic acid. As the cells respire anaerobically, the amount of lactic acid in the muscle increases and makes it ache. The lactic acid is broken down in the liver after being carried there in the blood.

Using anaerobic respiration

Yeast respires anaerobically to produce alcohol and carbon dioxide. It is used to make bread and alcoholic drinks.

Bread is made by mixing flour, water, yeast and sugar into a grey–white lump called dough. Inside the dough the yeast respires anaerobically and produces bubbles of carbon dioxide that make the dough rise. In a bakery the dough is cut into pieces to make loaves. Each piece of dough is put into a baking tin. When bubbles of gas are heated they expand, so the tins are kept in a warm cupboard for about half an hour to allow the dough to rise even more. They are then placed in an oven for baking. The alcohol evaporates in the heat and a loaf, with a spongy texture, is produced.

Yeast and sugar are used as ingredients to make alcoholic drinks, such as wine and beer. The process of producing alcohol for drinks is called fermentation. During this process bubbles of carbon dioxide are also produced. The alcohol produced mixes with the water in the drink. Alcohol is a poison, so fermentation must be regulated to prevent it increasing to concentrations that kill the yeast. If fermentation was allowed to continue until it stopped, a solution of about 14% alcohol would be produced.

19 How does yeast make the spongy texture of the bread?
20 Why does the dough rise even more in a warm oven?
21 Why does fermentation not produce a stronger alcoholic solution than about 14%?

Respiratory system

The function of the respiratory system is to provide a means of exchanging oxygen and carbon dioxide that meets the needs of the body, whether it is active or at rest. In humans the system is located in the head, neck and chest. It can be divided into three parts – the air passages and tubes, the pump that moves the air in and out of the system and the respiratory surface. The terms respiration and breathing are often confused but they do have different meanings. Breathing just describes the movement of air in and out of the lungs. Respiration covers the whole process by which oxygen is taken into the body, transported to the cells and used in a reaction with glucose to release energy, with the production of water and carbon dioxide as waste products.

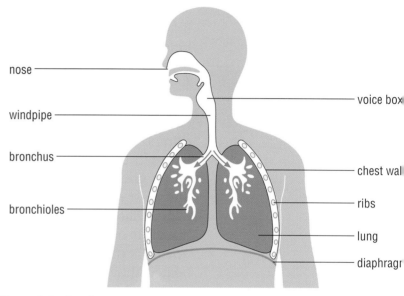

Figure 4.8 Respiratory system.

Air passages and tubes

Nose

Air normally enters the air passages through the nose. Hairs in the nose trap some of the dust particles that are carried on the air currents. The lining of the nose produces a watery liquid called mucus. This makes the air moist as it passes inwards and also traps bacteria that are carried on the air currents. Blood vessels beneath the nasal lining release heat that warms the air before it passes into the lungs.

Windpipe

The windpipe or trachea is about 10 cm long and 1.5 cm wide. It is made from rings of cartilage which is a fairly rigid substance. Each ring is in the shape of a 'C'. The inner lining of the windpipe has two types of cells. They are mucus secreting cells and ciliated epithelial cells. Dust particles and bacteria are trapped in the mucus. The cilia beat backwards and forwards to move the mucus to the top of the windpipe where it enters the back of the mouth and is swallowed.

22 What structures hold the air
passages open in the windpipe
and bronchi?

23 Why is it more difficult to
breathe during an asthmatic
attack?

Bronchi and bronchioles

The windpipe divides into two smaller tubes called
bronchi. (This is the name for more than one tube. A
single tube is called a bronchus.) The two bronchi are
also made of hoops of cartilage and have the same lining
as the windpipe.

The bronchi divide up into many smaller tubes called
bronchioles. These have a diameter of about 1 mm. The
bronchioles divide many times. They have walls made of
muscle but do not have hoops of cartilage. The wall
muscles can make the bronchiole diameter narrower or
wider.

Some people suffer from asthma. They may be allergic
to certain proteins in food or to the proteins in dust that
come from fur and feathers. The presence of these
proteins in the air affects the muscles in the bronchioles,
and the air passages in the bronchioles become
narrower. This makes breathing very difficult. A person
suffering an asthmatic attack can use an inhaler that
releases chemicals to make the muscles relax to widen
the bronchioles.

Air pump

The two parts of the air pump are the chest wall and the
diaphragm. They surround the cavity in the chest. Most
of the space inside the chest is taken up by the lungs.
The outer surfaces of the lungs always lie close to the
inside wall of the chest. The small space between the
lungs and the chest wall is called the pleural cavity. The
cavity contains a film of liquid that acts like a lubricating
oil, helping the lung and chest wall surfaces to slide over
each other during breathing.

24 Why is there a film of liquid in
the pleural cavity?

Chest wall

This is made by the ribs and their muscles. Each rib is
attached to the backbone by a joint that allows only a
small amount of movement. The muscles between the
ribs are called the internal and external intercostal
muscles. The action of these muscles moves the ribs.

Diaphragm

This is a large sheet of muscle attached to the edges of
the 10th pair of ribs and the backbone. It separates the
chest cavity, which contains the lungs and heart, from
the lower body cavity, which contains the stomach,
intestines, liver, kidneys and female reproductive organs.

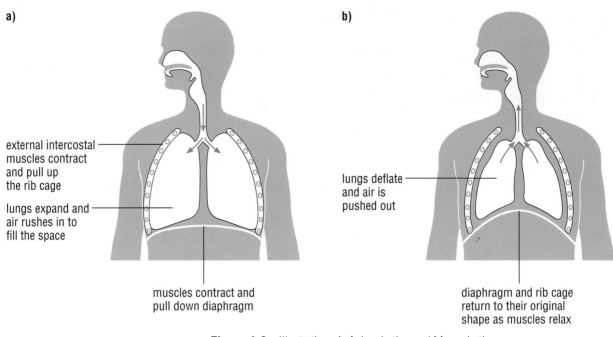

a)

external intercostal
muscles contract
and pull up
the rib cage

lungs expand and
air rushes in to
fill the space

muscles contract and
pull down diaphragm

b)

lungs deflate
and air is
pushed out

diaphragm and rib cage
return to their original
shape as muscles relax

Figure 4.9 Illustration of **a)** inspiration and **b)** expiration.

Breathing movements

There are two breathing movements called inspiration
and expiration.

Inspiration

During inspiration the external intercostal muscles
contract and the ribs move upwards and outwards. The
muscles of the diaphragm contract, pulling it down into a
flatter position. These actions increase the volume of the
chest and reduce the pressure of air inside it. Therefore,
air rushes in through the trachea and bronchi from
outside the body. It is pushed in by the pressure of the
air outside the body.

Expiration

The external intercostal muscles relax and the ribs fall
back into their original position. Gravity is the main force
that lowers the ribs and moves them inwards but the
weak internal intercostal muscles may also help when
they contract. The muscle fibres in the diaphragm relax
and it rises to its dome-shaped position again. The
organs below the diaphragm, which were pushed down
when the diaphragm muscles contracted, now push
upwards on the diaphragm. As the volume of the chest
decreases, the pressure of the air inside it increases and
air is pushed to the outside through the air passages.

25 How does the action of the external intercostal and diaphragm muscles draw air up your nose?

26 How do the values of the tidal volume and vital capacity compare?

27 A resting person gets up and starts running. Describe two ways in which the person's breathing pattern changes.

28 Why should a person's breathing pattern change between resting and running?

Depth of breathing

The amount of air breathed in and out at rest is called the tidal volume and is about 500 cm³ in humans. The maximum amount of air that can be breathed in and out is called the vital capacity. In human adults the vital capacity may reach 4000 cm³.

Respiratory surface

At the end of each bronchiole is a very short tube called the alveolar duct. Bubble-like structures called alveoli open into this duct. Each alveolus has a moist lining, a thin wall and is supplied with tiny blood vessels called capillaries.

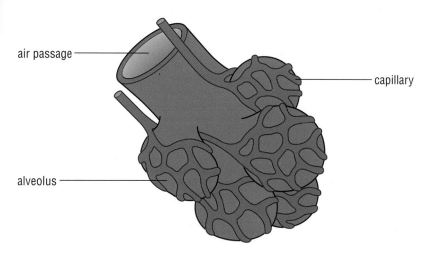

air passage

capillary

alveolus

Figure 4.10 An alveolus.

Oxygen from the inhaled air dissolves in the moist alveolar lining and moves by diffusion through the walls of the alveolus and the capillary next to it. The oxygen diffuses into the blood and enters the red blood cells (see page 49), which contain a dark red substance called haemoglobin. The oxygen then combines with the haemoglobin to make oxyhaemoglobin, which is bright red. Blood that has received oxygen from the air in the lungs is known as oxygenated blood.

Carbon dioxide is dissolved in the watery part of the blood called the plasma. It moves by diffusion through the capillary and alveolar walls and changes into a gas as it leaves the moist lining of the alveolus.

Blood moves through the capillaries very quickly, so a large amount of oxygen and carbon dioxide can be exchanged in a short time.

The spongy structure of the lungs is produced by the 300 million alveoli which make a very large surface area through which the gases can be exchanged. It is like having the surface area of a tennis court wrapped up inside two footballs! If this surface area is reduced then health suffers (see Smoking and health, page 72).

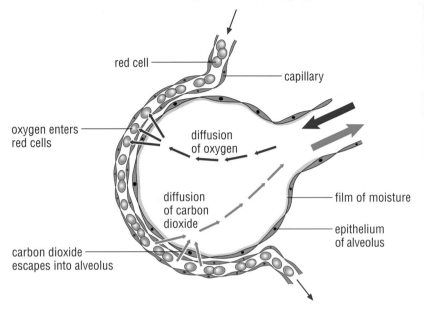

Figure 4.11 Diagram to show the direction of gaseous exchange.

Testing for carbon dioxide

Exhaled air can be tested for carbon dioxide by passing it through limewater. If carbon dioxide is present it reacts with the calcium hydroxide dissolved in the water to produce insoluble calcium carbonate. This makes the water turn white or milky.

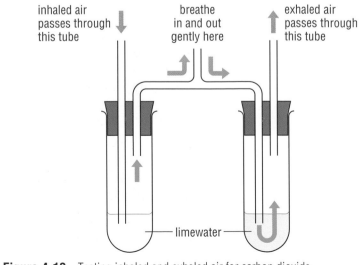

29 How would thick-walled alveoli affect the exchange of the respiratory gases?

30 Compare the way the blood carries oxygen and carbon dioxide.

31 How do you think you would be affected if the surface area of your lungs was reduced?

Figure 4.12 Testing inhaled and exhaled air for carbon dioxide.

Circulatory system

There are between 5 and 6 litres of blood in an adult. It flows through 100 000 km of tubes called blood vessels.

What is in the blood?

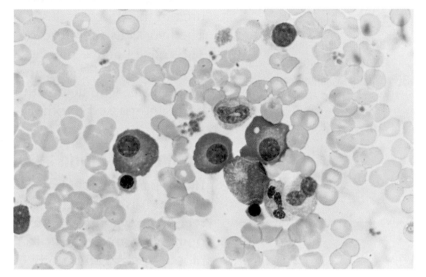

Figure 4.13 Blood cells and platelets.

About 45% of a drop of blood is made from cells. There are two kinds, red cells and white cells.

Red cells contain haemoglobin which transports oxygen from the lungs to the other body cells. Haemoglobin allows the blood to carry 100 times more oxygen than the same amount of water. There are 500 red cells for every white cell.

White cells fight disease. They attack bacteria and produce chemicals to stop viral infections (see page 64). White cells also gather at the site of a wound where the skin has been cut. They eat bacteria that try to enter. The white cells die in this process and their bodies collect to form pus in the wound.

The blood also carries platelets which are fragments of cells. These collect in the capillaries at the site of a wound and act to block the flow of blood. Platelets help the blood to form clots at the site of a wound. These clots stop blood leaking out of the wound.

About 55% of blood is a watery liquid called plasma. This contains digested foods, hormones, such as adrenaline (see page 2), a waste product from the liver called urea and the carbon dioxide produced by all the body cells.

32 Could you live without haemoglobin? Explain your answer.

33 Compare the tasks of red and white blood cells.

34 What does a typical body cell, such as a skin cell, receive from the blood and what does it give to the blood?

35 What does a liver cell give to the blood?

Chemical reactions in all cells produce heat. For example, it has been estimated that at least 500 different chemical reactions take place in the liver because it does so many tasks. These tasks include controlling the amount of sugar in the blood by storing it or releasing it; breaking down unwanted amino acids and producing urea in the process; destroying poisons, and making bile. The liver cells therefore produce large amounts of heat. The cells of active muscles also produce large amounts of heat. Blood receives and carries this heat as it passes by the cells. The heat is then transported around the body and passed to other less active cells, keeping them warm.

Path of the blood

Blood passes through the heart twice in the circulatory system. It is pumped from the heart to the lungs where it receives oxygen, then travels back to the heart. It is then pumped from the heart to the body. Oxygen from the blood passes to the body cells and carbon dioxide enters the blood from the body cells before returning to the heart. As individual blood cells travel around the body they usually pass through just one organ (such as the brain or the stomach or the kidney) before returning to the heart. They are then pumped to the lungs before going to the body again. It only takes about 45 seconds for a blood cell to travel around the circulatory system one time.

36 How does the blood change as it passes through the **a)** small intestine, **b)** lung, **c)** liver and **d)** brain?

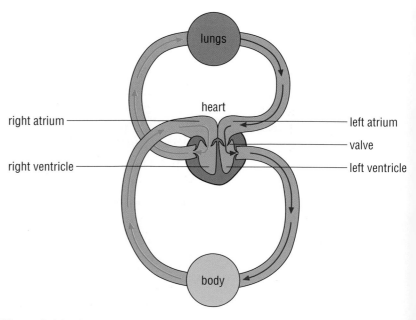

Figure 4.14 A simplified path of the blood through the circulatory system.

Blood vessels

Arteries

Blood vessels that take blood away from the heart are called arteries. The high pressure of blood pushes strongly on the thick, elastic artery walls. They stretch and shrink as the blood moves by. This movement of the artery wall makes a pulse. When an artery passes close to the skin the pulse can be felt and therefore used to count how fast the heart is beating.

Veins

Blood vessels that bring blood towards the heart are called veins. The blood is not under such high pressure and so does not push as strongly on the vein walls. Veins have thinner walls than arteries and contain valves that stop the blood flowing backwards.

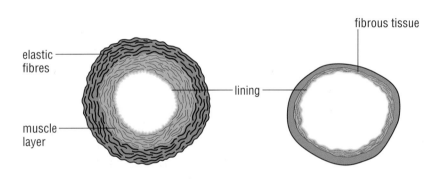

Figure 4.15 An artery and a vein.

Capillaries

When an artery reaches an organ it splits into smaller and smaller vessels. The smallest blood vessels are called capillaries. A capillary wall is only one cell thick. They are spread throughout the organ so that all cells have blood passing close to them. Where the blood leaves an organ, the capillaries join together to form larger and larger vessels until eventually they form veins.

Heart

Movement of the blood is produced by the pumping action of the heart. The heart is divided down the middle into two halves. The right side receives deoxygenated blood from the body and pumps it to the lungs. At the same time the left sides receives oxygenated blood from the lungs and pumps it to the body.

37 Why do veins have valves?
38 Why do you think arteries function better with thick walls?

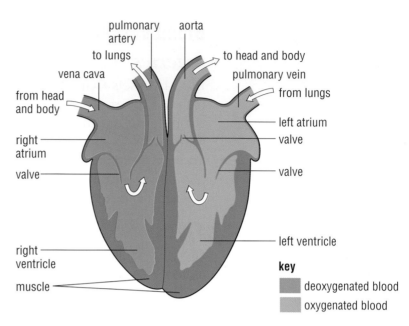

Figure 4.16   A simplified section through the heart.

Each side has two chambers. Blood flows from the veins into the upper chambers called the atria (*singular*: atrium). It passes from the atria into the lower chambers, the ventricles. The muscular walls of the ventricles relax as they fill up. When these muscular walls contract the blood is pumped into the arteries. Valves between the atria and the ventricles stop the blood going backwards into the atria. Valves between the main artery (aorta) and the ventricles stop the blood from flowing backwards after it has been pumped out of the heart.

The two pumps in the heart and a simplified arrangement of the blood vessels are shown in Figure 4.16. The structure of the heart with the two pumps is shown more realistically in Figure 4.17.

39 Where does the pushing force come from to push the blood out of the heart?

40 What is the purpose of the heart valves?

41 Why do you think the walls of the left ventricle are thicker than the walls of the right ventricle?

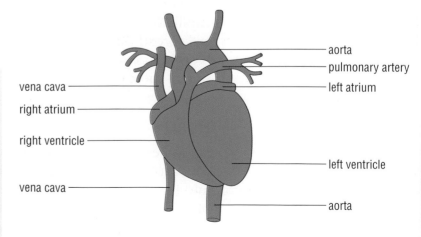

Figure 4.17   The structure of the heart.

Studies on the circulatory system

Erasistratus (about 304 BC–250 BC) was a Greek doctor who studied the circulatory system. He suggested that veins and arteries carried different substances. He thought that veins carried blood and arteries carried 'animal spirit'.

Galen (about AD 200–AD 130) was also a Greek doctor. He used the pulse of a patient to help him to assess their sickness. He realised that the blood from one side of the heart got to the other side but he did not know how it happened. He thought there were tiny holes in the wall between the two sides of the heart. Galen also thought that the blood went backwards and forwards along the blood vessels. His ideas were held in high regard for over 1400 years.

Michael Servetus (1511–1553) was a Spanish doctor who traced the path of blood to and from the heart along the vein and artery that go to and from the lungs. He did not think that the blood went into the heart's muscular walls.

Fabricius ab Aquapendente (1537–1619) was a professor of surgery who discovered that the veins had valves in them. He taught the Englishman William Harvey (1578–1657) who became a doctor and went on to do further studies of the circulatory system. Fabricius's discovery of the valves gave Harvey a clue as to how the blood might flow. He followed up Fabricius's discovery by blocking an artery by tying a cord around it. He found that the side towards the heart swelled up because of the collecting blood. Next, he tied a cord around a vein. He found that the vein swelled on the side away from the heart.

Harvey also calculated the amount of blood that the heart pumped out in an hour. It was three times the weight of a man, yet the body did not increase in size. One explanation was that the heart made this amount of blood in an hour and another organ in the body destroyed it so the body did not increase in size. Harvey thought it impossible for the blood to be made and destroyed so quickly and so suggested that the blood must move around the body in only one direction. He published his ideas in a book in 1628 and was ridiculed by other doctors for challenging the ideas of Galen. Eventually the idea of the blood circulating round the body was accepted but Harvey could not explain how the blood got from the arteries to the veins.

Marcello Malpighi (1628–1694) was an Italian scientist who studied the wing of a bat with a microscope. He found that there was a connection between the arteries and veins in the wing. These were tiny vessels that could not be seen with the eye. These vessels were called capillaries and the blood could be seen flowing through them.

1 Who first described arteries and veins?
2 Who first began to doubt Galen's ideas?
3 How did Fabricius's discovery help Harvey?
4 If the blood flowed as Galen suggested what would Harvey have found when he tied off the artery and vein?
5 How did Harvey interpret his observations?
6 Why was Harvey's idea ridiculed?
7 How did Malpighi's work support Harvey's ideas?

Figure A William Harvey at work.

◆ SUMMARY ◆

- Bones of the skeleton support the soft tissues of the body and provide protection for some organs (*see page 37*). There are joints between the bones which allow movement (*see page 38*).
- Muscles provide the power for movement when they contract (*see page 38*).
- The action of the muscles is co-ordinated by the central nervous system (*see page 40*).
- A stimulus causes a sensory cell to send a message to the brain (*see page 40*).
- The reflex response is the simplest response to a stimulus (*see page 41*).
- Energy is released from food in respiration (*see page 42*).
- In aerobic respiration oxygen is used to release energy from food (*see page 42*).
- In anaerobic respiration energy is released from food without the use of oxygen (*see page 43*).
- Oxygen and carbon dioxide are exchanged in the respiratory system (*see page 43*).
- Breathing is the process of air exchange between the air and lungs (*see page 44*).
- Breathing movements, inspiration and expiration, are caused by the movement of the chest wall and the diaphragm (*see page 46*).
- Blood is composed of the plasma, cells and platelets (*see page 49*).
- Blood moves along two distinct paths in the circulatory system (*see page 50*).
- The three kinds of blood vessels are arteries, veins and capillaries (*see page 51*).
- The heart contains two pumps for moving blood (*see page 52*).

End of chapter question

For discussion

Luigi Baglivi (1668–1707) was an Italian doctor who believed that the body is just a machine. He matched scissors to teeth, bones to levers and lungs to bellows.

a) If he had been alive today what may he have matched the brain to?

b) Was he right to think of the body as just a machine?

5 Keeping healthy

A body is made up of billions of cells. Groups of similar cells form tissues that work together with other tissues in larger structures called organs. The organs form groups called organ systems (see page 1) which work together to keep the body alive. The power to make the organ systems work comes from the energy in food, which is released by chemical reactions. The way the body is made and the way it works are incredibly complicated. If you live a healthy lifestyle and have a healthy diet (see page 21) your body may keep working for over 80 years. If you live an unhealthy lifestyle the cells, tissues and organs may become damaged.

Figure 5.1 A family enjoying a balanced meal.

Exercise

Regular exercise makes many of the organ systems become more efficient. It also uses up energy and helps to prevent large amounts of fat building up in the body. Exercise can increase your fitness in three ways: it can improve your strength, make your body more flexible and less likely to suffer from sprains, and it can increase your endurance which is your ability to exercise steadily for long periods without resting. Different activities require different levels of fitness. Table 5.1 shows these levels for different sporting activities. By studying the table you can work out which activities you could do to develop one or more of the three components of fitness.

1 Which activities demand great flexibility?
2 Which activity is the least demanding?
3 Which activities are the most demanding?
4 How do the demands of soccer and long distance running compare?
5 Which activity would you choose from the table? What are its strengths and weaknesses?
6 Many people claim that they do not have time to exercise. How would you motivate such people to take some form of exercise? Which activities might suit them best?

Table 5.1

Activity	Strength	Flexibility	Endurance
Basketball	xx	xx	xxx
Dancing	xx	xxx	xx
Golf	xx	xx	xx
Long distance running	xxx	xx	xxx
Soccer	xx	xx	xxx
Squash	xxx	xxx	xxx
Swimming	xxx	xx	xxx
Tennis	xxx	xxx	xxx
Walking	x	x	xx

Heart disease

The human heart starts to form in the embryo 20 days after conception (see page 91). Fewer than 1% of babies are born with heart defects, yet in the United Kingdom more people die from heart disease than from any other disease.

The heart may beat up to 2500 million times during a person's life. Its function is to push blood around the 100 000 km of blood vessels in the body. This push creates a blood pressure that drives the blood through the blood vessels. As the ventricles in the heart fill with blood the pressure in the blood vessels is reduced, but as the heart pumps it out along the arteries the blood pressure rises. The walls of the arteries are elastic and they stretch and contract with the blood pressure. In young people the artery walls are clear and their diameters are large enough to let the blood flow with ease. As the body ages the artery walls become less elastic.

The heart has its own blood vessels called the coronary arteries and veins. They transport blood to and from the heart muscle.

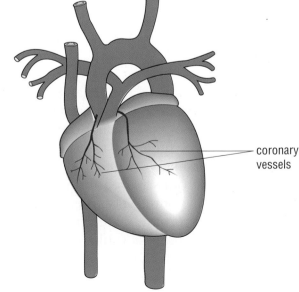

coronary vessels

Figure 5.2 The coronary blood vessels.

Fatty substances, such as cholesterol, stick to the walls of arteries. Calcium settles in the fatty layer and forms a raised patch called an atheroma. The blood then has less space to pass along the arteries and its pressure rises as it pushes through the narrower tubes. Other components of the blood, such as platelets, settle on the atheroma and make it larger. This may cause a blood clot which narrows the artery even more or can completely block it causing a thrombosis. This means that the artery is unable to supply oxygen and other nutrients to the relevant organ. A thrombosis in a coronary artery causes a heart attack. A thrombosis in an artery in the brain causes a stroke.

The features that develop in the body that cause heart disease can be inherited. People whose relatives have suffered from heart disease should take special care to keep their heart and circulatory system healthy.

Keeping the heart healthy

The heart is made of muscle and like all muscles it needs exercise if it is to remain strong. The heart muscles are exercised when you take part in the activities in Table 5.1. Heart muscle contracts faster and more powerfully during exercise than it does at rest so that more blood can be pumped to your muscles. These muscles need more blood to provide extra oxygen while they work (see also page 43).

As we have seen, the blood supply to heart muscles can be reduced by fatty substances such as cholesterol in the blood. These substances are formed after the digestion of fatty foods. Some fatty substances are needed to keep the membranes of the cells healthy, but too much intake of fat leads to heart disease. A heart can be kept healthy by cutting down on the amount of fat in the diet. This may be achieved by cutting fat off meat, or eating fewer crisps and chips for example.

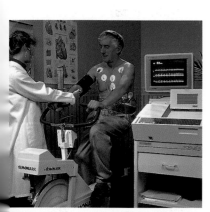

Figure 5.3 Pedalling an exercise bicycle makes the heart beat faster to provide blood for the leg muscles.

Microorganisms

Nowadays, most people enjoy good health most of the time but in the past many diseases were common. This improvement in health is mainly due to investigations that were carried out on microorganisms and disease in the 19th Century. Before that time microorganisms were thought to be produced by decaying substances, such as the remains of dead plants and animals. One of the early investigations of Louis Pasteur showed that the opposite happened – the microorganisms caused the decay.

Pasteur went on to develop his 'germ theory'. He thought that diseases might be caused by microorganisms and that disease might be spread by touch, the droplets of mucus forced in the air by a sneeze and by faeces. He and other scientists performed a large number of investigations which showed the 'germ theory' to be true. The microorganisms that cause disease are mainly bacteria or viruses.

Bacteria

Bacteria are single-celled organisms that range in size from 0.001 μm–0.5 μm. They can be seen using a light microscope.

Most bacteria feed on the remains of plants and animals or on animal waste. They feed by secreting a digestive juice which breaks down the food substances around them. Then they draw in the digested food substances for use in growth and reproduction.

Bacteria usually reproduce by a process called fission where each bacterium divides into two. If they have enough warmth, moisture and food, some bacteria can reproduce by fission once every 20 minutes. When conditions become dry or hot and unsuitable for feeding and breeding, some bacteria form spores. A spore has a thick wall which protects the bacterium from the hot, dry conditions. Bacteria can survive inside spores for a long time. They break out of the spores when favourable conditions return.

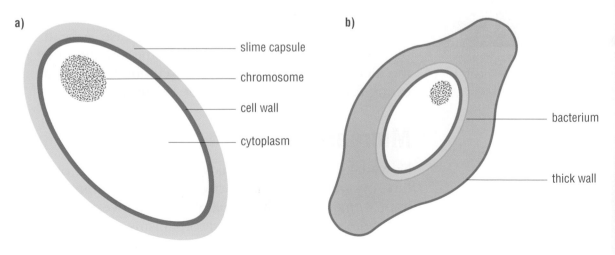

Figure 5.4 **a)** A bacterium and **b)** a bacterial spore.

Some, but not all, bacteria can cause disease. Diphtheria, whooping cough, cholera, typhoid, tuberculosis and food poisoning are all caused by different kinds of bacteria.

Viruses

Viruses are even smaller than bacteria. They are so small that they can only be seen with an electron microscope. Viruses do not show the characteristics of living things such as feeding, respiring or growing (see page 145). They are usually classified as non-living but they are able to reproduce if they enter a living cell. As they reproduce they destroy the cells they are in. Each kind of virus attacks certain cells in the body. For example, the cold virus attacks the cells that line the inside of the nose. The destructive action of the cold virus on the cells in the nose makes the nose run. In addition to the common cold, viruses can also cause influenza, chicken pox, measles and rabies and can lead to the development of AIDS (see page 85).

7 How are viruses and bacteria different?

8 Produce a table of diseases caused by viruses and bacteria.

9 If a bacterium could divide into two every 20 minutes how many bacteria would be produced after 8 hours?

The virus sticks to the membrane of a cell

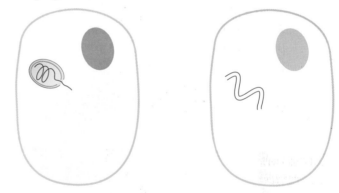

The virus enters the cell, the protein coat breaks down and releases the DNA

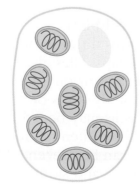

The viral DNA divides and directs the cell to make new protein coats

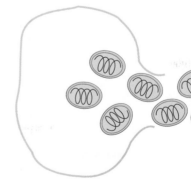

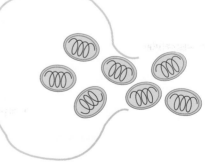

The cell wall breaks down to release the new viruses

Figure 5.5 How viruses reproduce.

Public health

In developed countries there are public health services that help to keep the population healthy. Two major features of the public health service are water treatment and waste disposal.

Water treatment

From the earliest times people have set up homes near sources of fresh water such as streams, rivers or lakes. They used the water for drinking, washing clothes, bathing and for taking away faeces and urine. In those days, though, people did not realise that there was a connection between using dirty water and diseases, such as typhoid and cholera.

Cleaning water to make it fit to drink and the treatment of waste water and sewage is expensive. These processes are only found widely in the wealthy developed countries. In many areas of developing countries there is not enough money available to provide these services and therefore people still suffer from diseases caused by microorganisms in the water. International aid programmes have been set up to help improve the water supplies in developing countries in order to reduce disease.

Figure 5.6 This pump is used to draw up water that has sunk into the ground and settled above water-resistant rocks.

Dangerous rubbish

Microorganisms thrive in decaying household waste such as kitchen scraps. Flies also breed in the waste and carry the microorganisms on their bodies when they leave the rubbish. If the fly lands on food left out in the kitchen microorganisms may be left behind to feed and breed. If the food is then eaten the microorganisms may cause illness. This can be prevented by storing rubbish in bins with secure lids and storing food in containers. In developed countries rubbish is collected from households and stored in tips under soil to reduce the spread of disease by flies and other pests such as rats.

Filtering bacteria

Many people have difficulty believing that the water they see raining onto a street may eventually come out of a tap and be clean enough to drink. This is made possible by passing the water through filters that remove harmful microorganisms.

In towns, rainwater runs off the street into the drains and through a series of pipes to the sewage works. The water entering a sewage works contains household waste and chemicals from factories as well as many harmful bacteria. It is first passed through a metal grid to remove large solid objects, such as bits of cloth or wood, before passing through a series of tanks. The other solid components of the sewage sink to the bottom of the first tank to form sludge. This is pumped into large containers called digesters where the disease-causing bacteria are destroyed by other microorganisms. The liquid that is left behind when the sludge is removed passes on to further tanks.

One of the ways this liquid is treated is to trickle it over a filter of clinkers. As the water splashes between the clinkers, oxygen in the air spaces kills some of the harmful bacteria. The remainder are destroyed by microorganisms that cover the surfaces of the clinkers. Afterwards the water may be released into a stream or river.

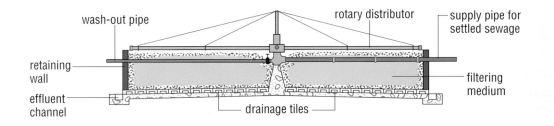

Figure A Sewage works filter.

If the river is long there may be a waterworks further down its length where water is extracted for a nearby town. In some areas, water entering a waterworks is first stored in reservoirs. It is at a waterworks that the water is made fit to drink. The water in a very large river may pass through the waterworks of several towns before it reaches the sea.

At a waterworks, gravel and grit are removed from the water by letting it settle. Then the bacteria are removed by passing the water through a sand filter. In the sand, harmless microscopic life forms a jelly-like substance through which the water passes. Protoctista (see page 144) in this layer feed on the harmful bacteria and remove them from the water. Chlorine or ozone is bubbled through the water at a later stage to kill any bacteria that might have passed through the filter.

Figure B Waterworks filters.

(continued)

The development of sewage systems

The first humans lived in small groups and moved through their environment hunting animals and gathering fruits and roots. They left their wastes such as urine and faeces behind them. The wastes were washed away into the soil by rain. When these people needed water they took it from the unpolluted streams and rivers as they moved along. When people began farming they stayed in one place. Farming provided a more regular food supply than hunting and gathering and the people became better fed, lived longer and had more children. As the human population increased many people settled in towns and cities. Human waste collected in the streets of these settlements and contaminated the drinking water. Diseases such as cholera and dysentery were common.

The first sewage system to remove human waste was set up 4500 years ago in a city called Mohenjo-Daro in the country that is now called Pakistan. There was a bathroom and toilet in every house in the city and the waste from them travelled in earthenware pipes to larger pipes that ran underneath the streets. The city was built on a huge mound of earth and was surrounded by fields on a plain through which the River Indus flowed. The sewage moved through the larger pipes to the edge of the city where it flowed into the fields.

About 2500 years ago, the Romans tackled the problem of removing sewage in Rome by building a system of drains. The main drain that connected the city centre to the River Tiber is still used today.

The Incas, living over 1000 years ago, also tackled the problem of sewage. In the city of Cuzco, which is now in Peru, they built some stone drains leading out of every home. The sewage was flushed away by water from mountain streams.

The people in the Ashanti kingdom in West Africa built drainage systems into their larger buildings 200 years ago. The wastes were carried by the drains to a river that carried them away from the settlement. Every day the drains were cleaned by pouring boiling water into them. In all the smaller settlements a public toilet was set up to prevent waste collecting in the streets.

Sewage systems were not developed in modern European cities until the end of the 19th Century. At first the sewage was moved along the drains to a river where it was released. In time the rivers became very polluted. By then scientists had learned a great deal about microorganisms, and in 1914 a sewage works was opened in Manchester (United Kingdom) which treated sewage with microorganisms to make it less harmful.

1 What are the ways in which harmful bacteria in water may be destroyed?
2 In which countries did the early sewage systems develop?
3 What materials were used in these systems?
4 What is the advantage of using mountain streams in a sewage system?
5 How could the use of boiling water affect microorganisms in the drains?
6 What is the purpose of a sewage system?

Figure A A Roman drain.

Figure B An Ashanti village.

Personal hygiene

During the course of the day sweat wells up from the pores in the skin. The water in the sweat evaporates to cool the body but other substances, such as urea, are left behind. Dirt sticks to the skin and dead skin cells flake off and join the dirt. Bacteria from the dirt or from the air feed and breed on these substances on the skin surface. Their activities make the skin smell and, if the skin is cut, they can enter the body and cause disease. Body odours caused by bacteria on the skin and the risk of infection are greatly reduced by a high standard of personal hygiene. This involves regular, thorough washing of skin and hair, regular changing and washing of clothes, particularly underclothes which are next to the skin, and regular tooth-brushing.

Acne

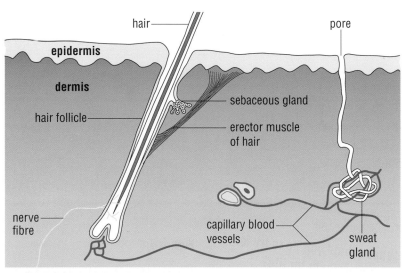

Figure 5.7 Hair follicle in the skin.

Hair grows out of tubes in the skin called follicles. There is a sebaceous gland in each follicle that secretes sebum. This substance prevents the skin becoming dry and gives it a waterproof coat. At puberty (see page 80) the body increases the production of sex hormones which may cause an increase in sebum production. The sebum can block the hair follicle and form a blackhead. Bacteria close by may breed and cause the skin to become inflamed to form a spot or pimple. Large numbers of pimples are called acne. In severe acne parts of the sebaceous glands are destroyed and cavities form in the skin. These can leave a scar.

10 Why should you clean your skin?

Microorganisms on teeth

If teeth are not cleaned regularly a sticky layer builds up on the enamel. This layer is called plaque and bacteria will settle in it. They feed on the sugar in food and make an acid. This breaks down the enamel and creates a cavity that may extend through the dentine into the pulp cavity. This has nerves running through it, so the tooth may become very sensitive, especially to hot or cold food and drink. If the cavity is not treated an abscess can form.

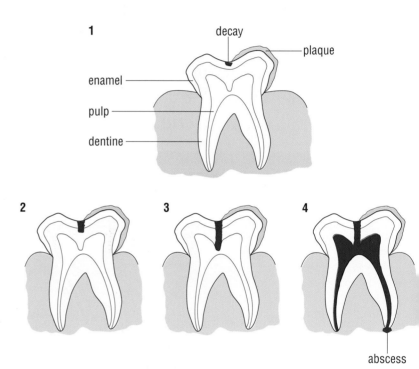

Figure 5.8 Stages in tooth decay.

For discussion
What should you do to try to keep your teeth for life?

How the body fights harmful microorganisms

The body's immune system acts to destroy harmful microorganisms. Most microorganisms are killed by white blood cells as they try to enter or soon after they enter the body through a cut, before they do any harm. These white blood cells are a type known as phagocytes. If the microorganisms do enter the blood and move round the body they come into contact with another type of white blood cell, known as lymphocytes. Microorganisms have chemicals called antigens on the surface of their bodies. Lymphocytes detect the antigens and make antibodies to attack the microorganisms and begin to destroy them. The destruction is completed by phagocytes that engulf the attacked microorganisms.

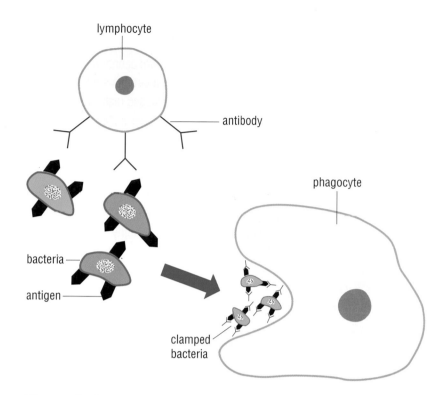

Figure 5.9 Destroying microorganisms in the body.

Each kind of microorganism has its own antigen which is different from any other. When the lymphocytes make an antibody to destroy an antigen it can attack only the particular kind of microorganism that makes that antigen. For example, the antibody that helps destroy the bacterium that causes whooping cough will not destroy the bacterium that causes diphtheria.

After a particular kind of disease-causing microorganism has been destroyed, the antibodies remain in the blood for some time. If reinfection occurs, the antibodies can destroy the invading microorganisms quickly before they build up into large numbers to cause disease. Even when the antibodies have left the blood the lymphocytes are quick to detect the antigens of the reinvading microorganism and make antibodies rapidly to begin the destruction process. The action of the lymphocytes gives the body immunity to the disease if the microorganism should reinfect it. The immunity that develops after the body has been infected with the disease-causing microorganism is called natural acquired immunity. In the past, all the immunity that a person had was built up in this way. Today, we are made immune from many microorganisms by a process called artificial immunisation.

Development of immunisation

The process of immunisation was developed by Edward Jenner in 1796. Smallpox was a common disease. It was caused by a virus that infected the respiratory system then moved to the skin where it caused rashes, spots and scabs full of pus that were called pustules. Fever also developed and death often followed.

Up until that time a process called variolation had been used to try and give protection from smallpox. This had been developed in China where it was first noticed that people with a mild form of smallpox survived and did not get it again. Pus was taken from their sores and was put in the skin or up the noses of healthy people who had not had smallpox. It was thought that they too should get a mild form of the smallpox and survive. Some people did survive but many developed the virulent form and died. However, in the absence of any better process the practice of variolation was passed on to Turkey and then moved into Europe.

Edward Jenner discovered that in a village where a smallpox outbreak occurred, the milk maids remained unharmed. He found that cattle suffered from a disease similar to smallpox but its effects were milder. When the milk maids milked the cattle they became infected with cowpox. Jenner thought that it gave them protection against smallpox.

Jenner planned an experiment to test his idea by adapting the practice of variolation. He took pus from the scabs of a person who had suffered from cowpox and put it into two cuts in the arm of an 8-year-old boy. The boy developed cowpox but quickly recovered. Seven weeks later Jenner took some pus from the scab of a smallpox patient and put some of the pus in the cuts. The boy did not get smallpox. Jenner called this process vaccination after the Latin word for cowpox 'vaccinia'. Soon vaccination was widely practised. Today no-one suffers from smallpox.

Fifty years after Jenner's experiment, Pasteur discovered a way of making sheep immune to anthrax. There is no mild form of anthrax so Pasteur looked at ways of weakening the microorganisms that produced the fatal disease. He discovered that if the microorganisms were heated then given to sheep they produced a mild form of the disease. When sheep recovered he gave them the normal microorganisms but they did not develop the fatal form of the disease. Weakened or attenuated microorganisms are used in immunisation schemes today.

1 What was the main problem with variolation?
2 What could have happened if Jenner had not been right?

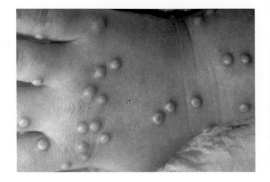

Figure A   The hand of a smallpox victim.

Artificial acquired immunity

The body can be made immune from infection without it having to suffer the full effects of the disease. This is done by vaccination. The body is injected with material that stimulates the lymphocytes to produce antibodies ready to attack those particular microorganisms if they infect the body in the future. The material that is injected may be one of the following.

1 Living microorganisms that have been weakened so that they cannot cause the disease before the lymphocytes produce antibodies to destroy them. The microorganisms that produce poliomyelitis, smallpox and tuberculosis are used for vaccination in this form.
2 Dead microorganisms. Their bodies still have the antigens that stimulate the lymphocytes to produce antibodies. The microorganisms that produce influenza, typhoid and whooping cough are used for vaccination in this form.
3 Poisonous toxins made by bacteria that have been treated to make them harmless. The toxins that cause diphtheria and tetanus are used for vaccination in this form.

While the immunity given by some vaccines can last a lifetime, other vaccines, such as those for cholera and typhoid, only give immunity for a certain length of time. Extra vaccinations, called boosters, are needed to keep the body immune from these diseases.

Passive immunity

The fetus developing in the womb does not make antibodies but receives some from the mother's blood through the placenta (see page 90). After the baby is born it may take in more antibodies through its mother's milk. Immunity built up in this way is called passive immunity. Soon the baby starts to make its own antibodies to build up immunity.

Building up protection

In the United Kingdom each young person is helped to build up immunity by receiving the series of vaccinations listed in Table 5.2 in their early life.

Immunisation against German measles (rubella) is provided to prevent the occurrence of rubella during pregnancy later in life. If a pregnant woman, who has not been immunised against German measles, is infected

11 What is the difference between
   a) an antibody and an antigen,
   b) a lymphocyte and a phagocyte?

12 How does the body fight reinfection
   a) shortly after it has recovered from the disease,
   b) a long time after it has recovered from the disease?

13 What are the benefits of artificial immunity?

14 How does society benefit from mass vaccinations against polio?

with the virus, it could also damage the tissues of the developing fetus. When born the baby may suffer deafness, mental handicap, disorders of the eyes and damage to the heart and liver.

Table 5.2 The immunisation schedule for children and young people in the United Kingdom.

Age	Immunisation
2 months	Diphtheria, tetanus, whooping cough, HIB, polio
3 months	Diphtheria, tetanus, whooping cough, HIB, polio
4 months	Diphtheria, tetanus, whooping cough, HIB, polio
12–18 months	Measles, mumps, rubella
4 years	Diphtheria, tetanus, whooping cough booster, measles, mumps, rubella
13–14 years	Tuberculosis (BCG)
15 years	Diphtheria, tetanus, polio

HIB = immunisation against *Haemophilus influenzae* type B disease, which can cause meningitis.

Operations today and yesterday

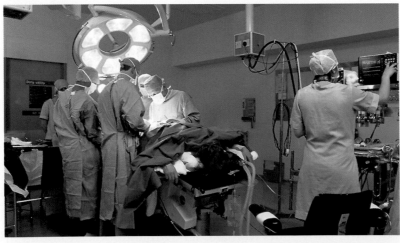

Figure A An operation in progress.

1 There is usually only one surgeon in a modern operating theatre. What do you think are the jobs of the other people in the room?
2 What differences can you see between the photograph of the modern operating theatre and the picture from Lister's time?

In this operation the surgeon cut open the patient's body to work on an organ inside. At the end of the operation the cut was stitched up and the patient returned to the ward for a few days before going home to make a full recovery. If microorganisms had entered the body during the operation they could have caused infections. They are prevented from doing so in the following ways. The air is filtered before it enters the operating theatre and the smooth easy-clean surfaces are washed with disinfectant. The instruments used in the operation and the caps, gowns and gloves of the people taking part are sterilised to kill any microorganisms that may have settled on them.

(continued)

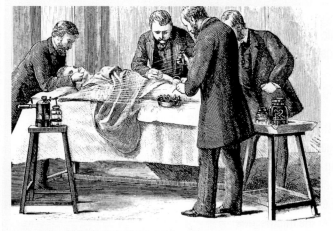

Figure B   Lister's carbolic spray in action.

3 What changes could the surgeons in Lister's day have made to help keep microorganisms from infecting the patient?

4 How did antiseptics get their name?

5 What do you do to prevent small wounds from becoming septic?

Joseph Lister (1827–1912) was a surgeon. In his day surgeons could perform successful operations but many of the patients died later because their wounds became infected and turned septic. When Lister heard about Pasteur's 'germ theory' he believed that microorganisms could be entering the patient's body during operations and causing the infections to develop. He decided to use a carbolic acid spray during his operations to kill any microorganisms that might be present. He found that his patients did not develop infections. Carbolic acid was the first antiseptic substance. Many more have been developed since Lister's time.

Fighting microorganisms with medicines

Bacteria can be destroyed with an antibiotic. Antibiotics are chemicals that are swallowed or injected to fight microorganisms inside the body. The antibiotic may stop the bacteria from making cell walls or it may affect the life processes taking place inside them. Two well known antibiotics are penicillin and tetracycline.

Viruses cannot be destroyed by antibiotics but some can be destroyed by antiviral drugs. A virus needs substances from the cell it has infected in order to reproduce. An antiviral drug stops the virus reaching these substances.

Antiseptics are chemicals used to attack micro-organisms on damaged skin and in the lining of the mouth. They are not swallowed. They are used as creams and mouthwashes.

Athlete's foot is a skin disease caused by a fungus. The fungus feeds on the damp skin between the toes of poorly dried feet. The disease can be cured by treating the feet with powder and cream containing a fungicide which kills the fungus.

15 What are the differences between an antibiotic and an antiviral drug?

The first antibiotic

Bacteria and fungi are two kinds of microorganisms which can be grown on plates of agar jelly that are sealed inside a petri dish. Agar jelly contains the nutrients that bacteria and fungi require.

In 1928 Alexander Fleming (1881–1955) was working in a laboratory when he noticed that a plate that had been set aside to grow colonies of a certain bacterium also had a green fungus growing on it. At first sight it looked as if the plate had been spoiled, but when Fleming looked again he saw that the bacterial colonies near to where the fungus was growing had been destroyed. He reasoned that there was a substance in the jelly, which had come from the fungus, that killed the bacteria. The fungus was called penicillium which means 'little brush'. It was given this name because under the microscope parts of the fungus look like little brushes. When Fleming extracted the substance from the fungus he called it penicillin.

Fleming tested penicillin on a range of bacteria and found that some were killed but others were not. He then tested penicillin on human white blood cells and found that they were not destroyed by concentrations that killed the bacteria. Fleming did not investigate penicillin further to discover its chemical structure, and when he published his work other scientists were not interested in it.

1 Why can bacteria and fungi grow well on agar?
2 Why was Fleming's agar plate thought to have been spoiled?
3 Why did Fleming believe the fungus made a substance that killed bacteria?
4 Look at Figure A. Which disc has the strongest antibiotic? Explain your answer.
5 How did the results of Fleming's experiment on human white blood cells suggest that penicillin could be useful?

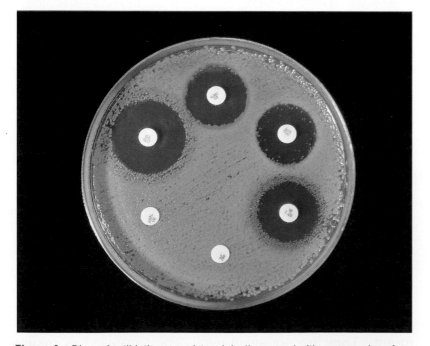

Figure A   Discs of antibiotics on a plate originally covered with a suspension of a bacterium called *Escherichia coli*. Plates of agar jelly containing bacterial colonies are still used to test antibiotics today.

(continued)

When the United Kingdom was preparing for World War II, a research programme was set up to find a substance that could be used to kill bacteria in soldiers' wounds. Ernst Chain (1906–1979) was working on the programme and looked up some work done by Fleming in 1922. In this work Fleming had discovered lysozyme, which is a chemical that kills bacteria and is found in tear drops. Chain also read about Fleming's discovery of penicillin. He told a scientist he was working with called Howard Florey (1898–1968) about it. Florey and Chain decided that penicillin could be the substance that was needed and began studying it in more detail. Their work led to penicillin being used to treat wounded soldiers in the war. In 1945 Fleming, Florey and Chain were awarded the Nobel Prize for Medicine.

Further investigations on penicillin continued during the war. They were made by Dorothy Hodgkin (1910–) who studied the crystal structure of chemicals by firing beams of X-rays at them. When the X-rays strike the chemical molecules they move off in new directions. These directions can be found by using a photographic film set-up around the chemical. The way to work out the structure of a molecule from the X-ray paths is very complicated and when Hodgkin used it to investigate penicillin she used a computer. This was the first time that a computer had been used in a biochemistry experiment. When Hodgkin had discovered the structure of penicillin she went on to investigate the structures of vitamin B_{12} and insulin. In 1964 she was awarded the Nobel Prize for Chemistry. The following year she was awarded the Order of Merit. The last woman to receive this award had been Florence Nightingale.

6 How did a bacteria-killing substance affect wounded soldiers?
7 How do you think penicillin affected the death rate in army hospitals?

Figure B Dorothy Hodgkin.

Drug abuse

Drugs are chemical substances that change the way we think, feel or behave. Some such as caffeine, which is found in tea and coffee, are made by plants. Medical drugs are usually made by the pharmaceutical industry from raw chemical materials. Most drugs are produced to ease the symptoms of a disease or to cure the disease. Although many people think of harmful drugs as being substances like heroin or cannabis, nicotine in cigarettes and alcohol in drinks like beer and wine are also drugs that can harm the body.

People begin taking harmful drugs for a variety of reasons. Some begin because they are unhappy, lonely or feel that they are unable to cope with life. They think the drugs will make them feel better. Others take them because their friends are trying them and they find it difficult to say no. Other people take them because they think it is exciting to use substances that are illegal. Whatever the reason, taking harmful drugs can be dangerous.

General body changes in drug abuse

A drug has an effect on how the body works. As a person continues to take certain drugs the body becomes more tolerant of them and larger amounts of the drug have to be taken for the person to feel its effects. The drug-taker's brain or body generally gets so used to the drug that it becomes changed in some way and becomes physically dependent on the drug. This is known as an addiction. If the person stops taking the drug the body reacts in a range of painful ways, including sickness. These reactions are called withdrawal symptoms.

While the body is becoming physically dependent on the drug, the person may be becoming psychologically dependent on it. This means that they become upset if they are not taking it and develop the irrational fear that they cannot cope with life without the drug.

Smoking and health

There are over a thousand different chemicals in cigarette smoke, including the highly addictive nicotine. These chemicals swirl around the air passages when a smoker inhales and touch the air passage linings. In a healthy person, dust particles are trapped in mucus and moved up to the throat by the beating of microscopic hairs called cilia. The small amounts of dust and mucus are then swallowed. In a smoker's respiratory system the cilia stop beating due to chemical damage by the smoke. More mucus is produced but instead of being carried up by the cilia it is coughed up by a jet of air as the lungs exhale strongly. This is a smoker's cough and the amount of dirty mucus reaching the throat may be too much to swallow.

In time chronic bronchitis may develop. The lining of the bronchi become inflamed and open to infection from microorganisms. The inflammation of the air passages makes breathing more difficult and the smoker develops a permanent cough. The coughing causes the walls of some of the alveoli in the lungs to burst. When this happens the surface area of the lungs in contact with the air is reduced. This leads to a disease called emphysema.

Some of the cells lining the air passages are killed by the chemicals in the smoke. They are replaced by cells below them as they divide and grow. Some of these cells may be damaged by the smoke too and as they divide they may form cancer cells. These cells replace the

16 What is the function of a smoker's cough?

17 Why may chronic bronchitis lead to other diseases?

18 How does the reduced number of alveoli affect the exchange of oxygen and carbon dioxide?

19 Why does someone with emphysema breathe more rapidly than a healthy person?

20 How are cancer cells different from normal cells in the lung tissue?

21 Why do cancer cells in an organ make the organ less efficient?

22 Why might the growth of cancer tumours in an organ have fatal results?

normal cells in the tissues around them but they do not perform the functions of the cells they replace. The cancer cells continue to divide and form a lump called a tumour. This may block the airway or break up and spread to other parts of the lung where they can set up more tumours.

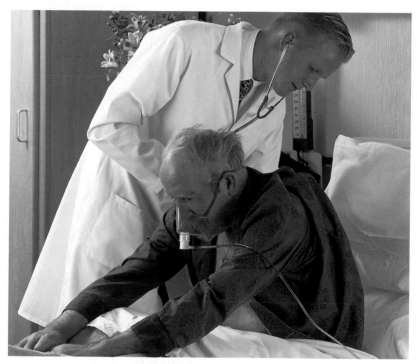

Figure 5.10 Effect of smoking on the respiratory system.

Alcohol

Many people have their first alcoholic drink at special family occasions such as birthdays and weddings. As they get older they may have a few drinks at weekends then perhaps during the week too. Drinking alcohol may be used at first as a form of relaxation with friends but may become a regular daily habit until the person cannot cope without drinking large amounts daily. This final stage is alcoholism. To avoid this people need to develop a sensible attitude towards alcohol.

Effect of alcoholic drinks

Alcohol affects the nervous system. It slows down the speed at which nerve cells carry signals. A small amount of alcohol may make a person feel more relaxed but it also makes the nerves work slightly slower. This makes a person react more slowly. As the person drinks more the effect of the alcohol on the nervous system increases and their reaction time becomes longer. The behaviour of the person may change. Their voice may become louder and they may become reckless and even aggressive. The person finds it more difficult to think and speak clearly. If they continue to drink their body movements may become unco-ordinated and the person may be unable to walk. They may fall asleep or become unconscious. In extreme cases, in the unconscious state they may be sick and if the vomit gets stuck in their windpipe they may suffocate and die.

Long term effects of alcohol abuse

Alcohol is a poison. The liver collects poisons from the blood as it flows through. It breaks down the poisons to make them harmless. If large amounts of alcohol are drunk over many years the liver may become inflamed and develop a disease called hepatitis. Parts of the liver may turn to scar tissue. This leads to the development of cirrhosis of the liver which reduces the liver's capacity to neutralise poisons. This disorder can be fatal.

Strength of alcoholic drinks

Bottles and cans of alcoholic drinks have the strength of their alcohol content marked on them. It is shown as a number with % ABV written after it. This means % alcohol by volume. Many beers have a strength of 3.5% ABV, while cans of lager or cider may be much stronger, having a strength of 9% ABV. Whisky may be 40% ABV, while sherry is about 15% ABV and wine about 11% ABV. Some 'alco-pops' may be up to 13.5% ABV.

Measures of alcohol

Alcohol is measured in units of pure alcohol. One unit is 8 g or 10 cm^3 of pure alcohol. To help people assess how much alcohol they are drinking the following three measures of drinks are used:

A half pint (284 ml) of 3.5% ABV beer = 1 unit
A 25 ml measure of a spirit drink such as whisky at 40% ABV = 1 unit
A 125 ml glass of wine at 8% ABV = 1 unit (most wines have a higher % ABV than 8%)

The number of units in a drink can be calculated by using this formula:

$$\frac{\text{Volume of drink}}{1000} \times \% \text{ ABV} = \text{number of units.}$$

23 Arrange wine, beer, 'alco-pops', whisky, sherry and cider in order of their alcoholic content, putting the strongest one first.

24 Do you think 'alco-pops' are suitable alcoholic drinks for young people? Explain your answer.

25 Calculate the units in these drinks:
   a) 440 ml can of lager at 4% ABV
   b) 500 ml can of cider at 9% ABV
   c) 20 cl bottle of 'alco-pop' at 13.5% ABV.

26 A man has two pints of beer in an hour and his wife has three glasses of wine. How long does it take their livers to destroy the alcohol they have drunk?

27 How long would it take a liver to destroy all the alcohol in a 75 cl 10% ABV bottle of wine?

Note: 1 cl = 10 ml.

For discussion

Would you be happy being driven by somebody who had recently drunk up to 5 units of alcohol?

Figure 5.11 Examples of drink units.

Using the measures to stay healthy

If people wish to drink and remain healthy they should not drink beyond a certain number of units of alcohol each week. For men the recommended limit is 21 units and for women the recommended limit is 14 units. The difference in limits is due to the size and water content of the body. Men are generally larger than women and have a higher water content. Between 55 and 65% of the body weight of a man is due to water, while water forms only between 45 and 55% of a woman's body weight.

Many countries have laws that aim to prevent people driving under the influence of alcohol. In the United Kingdom this limit is set at the amount of alcohol that gives a blood alcohol level of 35 mg/100 cm^3. The number of units that gives this blood alcohol level varies between different people but is about 3 units. In other countries the limit is less. Many people believe that no alcohol at all should be drunk before driving.

The liver and alcohol removal

It takes the liver about 1 hour to destroy 1 unit of alcohol. If a person drinks more than 1 unit in an hour, the concentration of alcohol in the blood increases and affects the rest of the body.

Solvents

When they are sniffed, the chemicals in a range of solvents can produce an effect similar to drunkenness. They cause the sniffer to have weird sensations that may be frightening or make them behave in a foolish or dangerous way.

The solvents that are sniffed are usually in certain kinds of glues, correcting fluids and aerosol sprays. The butane gas used as the fuel in cigarette lighters is also inhaled. The effect of a solvent on the body occurs very quickly because the chemicals enter the blood through the thin lining of the lungs. The effect does not last long. If a person wants to stay under the effect of the solvent he/she has to keep sniffing.

People react differently to the chemicals in solvents. Some young people have died after sniffing solvents for the first time. The solvents can damage lungs, the control of breathing, the nervous system, liver, kidneys and bone marrow. As sniffers lose control of themselves, they may suffocate on the plastic bags they use to inhale the solvent, become unconscious then be sick and suffocate in their vomit, or cause a fire and risk burning themselves when lighting a cigarette near solvents that are flammable.

Figure 5.12 A selection of booklets on help for drugs and solvent abuse.

Dangers of other drugs

Ecstasy

Ecstasy affects the body's co-ordination. It can make a person confused. It also acts as a stimulant and can seriously affect people who suffer from epilepsy or have a heart condition. It can be fatal.

Amphetamine or speed

Amphetamines are stimulants. Their use can lead to mental disorders and heart damage.

Cocaine and crack

Cocaine is sniffed or injected. Crack is a form of cocaine that can be smoked. Both are stimulants and are highly addictive. They can make users feel sick, itchy, suffer nose damage, have difficulty sleeping and develop mental disorders.

LSD (acid)

LSD affects the brain and makes the user see things that are not there. These illusions are called hallucinations. They may be frightening and lead to the person being upset when the effect has worn off. People who use LSD regularly can become less alert to the world around them.

Cannabis

Cannabis can produce hallucinations and make people upset. If it is smoked it can cause the same diseases as smoking tobacco.

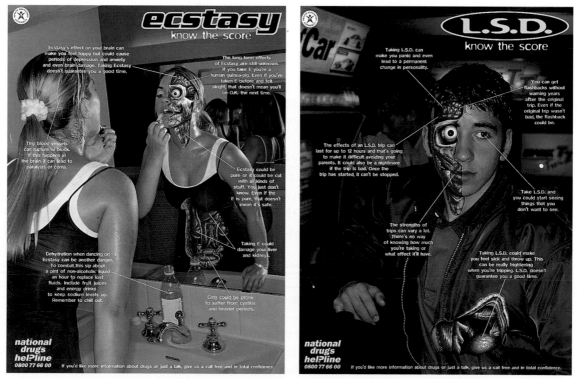

Figure 5.13 Posters to discourage drug taking.

Heroin

Heroin can make first-time users so sick that they will never try it again. Regular heroin users are physically and psychologically dependent on it and will commit crimes

For discussion

What might be the effect of making the drugs in this section legal?

How effective are posters at preventing drug abuse?

What else could be useful ?

to obtain money to buy more. They may have slurred speech and seem slightly sleepy. Heroin addicts who inject the drug are in danger of catching hepatitis and AIDS from sharing dirty needles. When heroin addicts try to give up the drug they have great difficulty losing their psychological dependence. They may still crave for the drug after they have stopped taking it for a long time.

◆ SUMMARY ◆

◆ Exercise makes many organs more efficient (*see page 55*).
◆ Heart disease is caused by eating an unhealthy diet, lack of exercise, or by features that are inherited from family members (*see page 57*).
◆ The main disease-causing microorganisms are viruses and bacteria (*see pages 58 and 59*).
◆ The body's immune system naturally helps destroy bacteria and viruses (*see page 64*).
◆ Water treatment is important for community health (*see page 60*).
◆ Skin hygiene and dental care are important components of personal hygiene (*see pages 63 and 64*).
◆ Immunity can be acquired artificially (*see page 67*).
◆ Medicines can be used to destroy microorganisms (*see page 69*).
◆ Smoking damages the bronchi and alveoli and can cause bronchitis, emphysema and cancer (*see page 72*).
◆ Alcohol abuse produces changes in behaviour that may be life-threatening. Prolonged abuse causes liver damage (*see page 75*).
◆ Solvents damage the lungs, nervous system, kidneys and bone marrow. They cause changes in behaviour that can be life-threatening (*see page 75*).
◆ Illegal drugs can cause damage to a wide range of body organs and can lead to mental disorders (*see pages 76–77*).

End of chapter questions

1 Explain why antibiotics cannot be used to cure the common cold.
2 How can microorganisms be used to keep us healthy?
3 How is someone putting their health at risk when they smoke tobacco daily and drink more than the recommended number of units of alcohol a week?
4 Some people have to inject themselves once a day to stay healthy. Can you think of a condition where this is the case and name the substance that is injected?
5 What is an ideal lifestyle for a healthy life?

6 Reproduction in humans

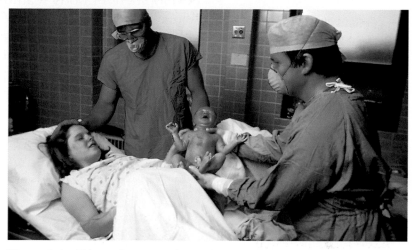

Figure 6.1 This new human was born only seconds ago.

How the changes begin

The bodies of newborn male and female babies are very similar. 'It's a girl!' or 'It's a boy!' can only be declared after looking at the baby's genitalia – the external parts of the reproductive organs. For about the next 10 years the bodies of boys and girls continue to be very similar (except for the genitalia), then changes begin.

Behind the nose and beneath the brain is an organ called the pituitary gland. This is one of several glands that secrete different hormones into the blood. A hormone is a chemical that is produced in one part of the body, circulates all round the body in the blood but only has an effect on a specific part of the body. At around the age of 10 to 13 in girls and 12 to 14 in boys, the pituitary gland secretes increased amounts of a hormone called growth hormone and another called gonadotrophin.

Growth hormone travels around the body and stimulates growth in the hands and feet, then the hips and chest, then causes the trunk followed by the legs to increase in length. These changes in body size can make people feel uncomfortable.

Gonadotrophin stimulates the production of sex hormones. In females sex hormones are produced in the ovaries. They produce two sex hormones called oestrogen and progesterone in large amounts. In males sex hormones are produced in the testes or testicles. They produce testosterone. The sex hormones cause the reproductive organs to develop fully and cause the development of body features known as secondary sexual characteristics. The sex hormones work with the growth hormone. In females they cause the hips to grow wider than the shoulders and to develop fat around them to give a smoother shape. In males testosterone causes the shoulders to grow wider and heavier than the hips.

Table 6.1 Secondary sexual characteristics.

Males	Females
Growth of hair on the face, armpits and pubic region	Growth of hair in armpits and pubic region
Voice becomes deeper	Breasts develop
Growth of penis and testicles	Growth of vagina and uterus
	Pelvis widens

Table 6.1 shows the secondary sexual characteristics that develop in males and females due to the action of these sex hormones. These changes take place over a period of about 3 years in girls but may take longer in boys. There is great variation in the time the changes begin and also in the nature and the size of the changes. These variations can make people unnecessarily anxious and cause them to worry if they feel they are not changing in the correct way. When the changes are complete each person is capable of reproduction. This period of change is called puberty. It takes place in the first half of adolescence, which is the time when a person changes from a child to an adult. In adolescence, in addition to becoming sexually mature, a person also develops adult emotions and social skills.

1 How may the body of a girl and a boy change from the beginning to the end of puberty?

2 Why do some people feel anxious as they go through puberty?

Figure 6.2 Most of the people in this school hall are going through puberty, while the rest went through puberty many years ago.

All mixed up

The greatest physical and emotional changes in a person's life take place during adolescence. At the end of this time people become adults, usually with a wider range of social skills to allow them to live independently, if they wish, and to develop their own ambitions for a happy life.

During adolescence people have to learn to cope with both the physical and emotional changes at once. In addition to the physical changes, girls have to learn to cope with periods (see page 83) and boys may have 'wet dreams' in which they release semen (see page 82) when they are asleep. A person's main emotional change is in wanting to be more independent and have more control over their lives. Generally, other members of the family adjust to these changes and the adolescent is allowed more freedom in choice of clothes and use of free time. Many schools also provide a wide range of sports, clubs and activities to help the adolescent to develop emotionally and socially.

It is natural for people in adolescence to be anxious sometimes and to worry whether they are going through the proper physical change. Some also try to be too independent too quickly. This may lead to arguments with parents and other adults. As well as seeking independence from their families they are also anxious not to lose their friends and may feel under pressure to follow the way their friends behave, even though they would prefer to do something else. The sex hormones also influence thoughts and make people interested in the opposite sex. The degree to which the sex hormones do this varies as much as the physical changes they make. All the changes taking place over a few short years sometimes make many adolescents feel confused. This is natural. Some people find that talking to others helps them cope, while other people feel embarrassed to talk about how they feel.

Figure A   A disco provides an opportunity to develop social skills.

For discussion

Is this a fair description of how people think and feel during adolescence?

What would you add to this account and what do you not agree with?

Male reproductive organs

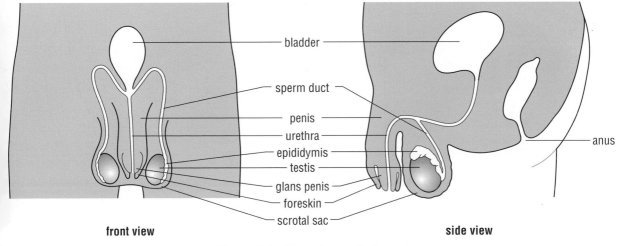

bladder

sperm duct

penis

urethra

epididymis

testis

glans penis

foreskin

scrotal sac

anus

front view

side view

Figure 6.3   The male reproductive system.

The testicles develop inside the body of the unborn child and usually move down to the outside of the body before the baby is born. The testicles are held in a bag of muscle and skin called the scrotum. They are positioned outside the body because the conditions are cooler there and are more favourable for sperm production. Each testicle contains long microscopic pipes called seminiferous tubules. The male gametes or sex cells are made inside these tubes. They are the sperm cells. On the top and side of each testicle is an epididymis. This is a long, coiled tube in which the sperm cells collect. The sperm cells travel to the outside of the body along the sperm duct and the urethra. There are glands along the path to the outside that add liquid to the sperm cells. The mixture of liquid is known as seminal fluid or semen.

The urethra runs through the middle of the penis. It is also connected to the bladder and is the tube through which the urine flows. Semen and urine do not flow down the urethra at the same time.

The penis contains spongy tissue along its length that can fill with blood to make it hard, stiff and erect (see pages 84 and 86). The tip of the penis, called the glans penis, has a large number of receptors and is very sensitive. The glans is covered with a fold of skin called the foreskin. If circumcision has taken place the foreskin will have been removed.

Female reproductive organs

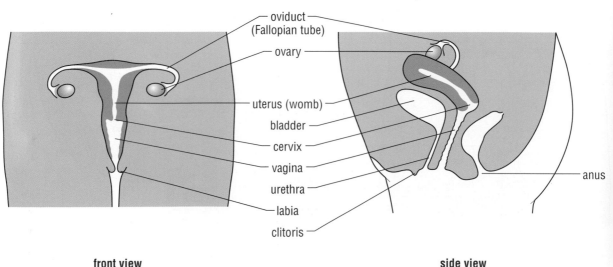

front view   side view

Figure 6.4   The female reproductive system.

The ovaries develop inside the body and, unlike the testicles, they stay there because egg production can take place at body temperature. Each ovary contains about 200 000 potential egg cells. Egg cells are the female gametes. Eggs are released as part of the menstrual cycle (see below). When an egg is released from an ovary it passes into the trumpet-shaped opening of the oviduct – a tube that connects to the uterus or womb. If an egg is fertilised (see page 87) it develops into a fetus in the uterus.

The uterus is connected to the vagina by the cervix. The vagina opens to the outside next to the opening of the urethra. Both openings are protected by folds of skin called labia. These folds also protect a region about the size of a small pea called the clitoris. This region has a large number of receptors like the tip of the penis.

Menstrual cycle

From the beginning of puberty the menstrual cycle occurs every month in females. It does not take place when the female is pregnant. It includes a period of bleeding from the vagina which may last for about 4 days. During this time an egg starts to mature in one of the ovaries. About 10 days after the period of bleeding ends, the egg, which is about the size of the dot on this i, escapes from the ovary. Alternate ovaries release an egg each month. The egg is then moved down the fluid-filled oviduct by the movement of cilia in the oviduct walls.

At the same time as the egg is maturing in the ovary, the uterus wall is thickening with blood. It does this to prepare to receive a newly formed embryo in case fertilisation takes place. The egg may survive for up to 2 days in the oviduct and fertilisation can take place during this time. If the egg is not fertilised no further development of the egg takes place. About 12 days after the egg dies, the uterus wall breaks down and blood passes out of the vagina. Another menstrual period begins.

The length of time of the period of bleeding varies between girls and so does the amount of blood that is released. Some girls and women feel ill a day or two before their period starts or feel pain for the first few days, while others are not affected in this way.

The menstrual cycle continues until the beginning of the menopause, which may start at about the age of 45. During the menopause periods may become irregular and eventually stop. The menopause may end when a woman is in her early 50s.

3 How are the male and female reproductive organs different?

4 How are they similar?

5 How long is the average menstrual cycle?

6 How does the wall of the uterus change during the course of the cycle and why?

7 What is the cause of the menstrual bleeding?

8 In what ways can periods vary?

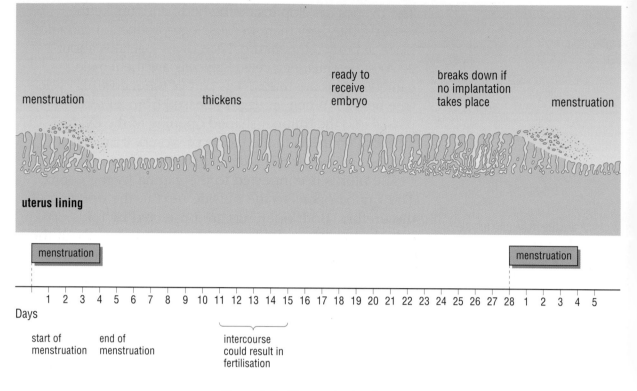

menstruation   thickens   ready to receive embryo   breaks down if no implantation takes place   menstruation

uterus lining

| menstruation | | menstruation |

Days

1 2 3 4 5 6 7 8 9 10 11 12 13 14 15 16 17 18 19 20 21 22 23 24 25 26 27 28 1 2 3 4 5

start of menstruation   end of menstruation   intercourse could result in fertilisation

Figure 6.5 The menstrual cycle.

Sexual intercourse

Before sexual intercourse can take place the penis must become erect. This happens by the action of a muscle at the base of the penis. It prevents the drainage of blood from the penis. The blood collects in the spongy tissue and makes it expand and become hard.

Prior to intercourse the vagina may also widen to ease the passage of the penis into it. The lining of the vagina may secrete a fluid that acts as a lubricant and further helps the penis to enter the vagina.

When the penis is inside the vagina both the male and female may make thrusting movements to stimulate the sensitive areas of the penis tip and the clitoris. This may give each partner a feeling of pleasure called an orgasm. When the male has an orgasm it is accompanied by a contraction of the muscles in the epididymis and sperm ducts which propels the semen through the penis into the vagina. The action of releasing the semen is called an ejaculation. The volume of semen ejaculated is usually about 3–5 cm^3.

Sexually transmitted diseases

Some diseases are transmitted by sexual intercourse. The main ones are gonorrhoea, syphilis, genital herpes and HIV, which leads to AIDS.

Gonorrhoea is caused by a bacterium. It infects the urethra in both sexes and the cervix in females. In males the infection causes pain when urinating and there is a discharge of pus from the penis. There may be no symptoms or pain in females. If not treated the infection can spread through the reproductive organs and cause sterility in both sexes. Gonorrhoea can be cured with antibiotics.

Syphilis is a disease that produces sores on the genitalia and later produces skin rashes, fever and headaches. If it is not treated with antibiotics at this stage, a final, incurable stage occurs. This may happen up to 20 years later and results in insanity, heart damage and death.

Genital herpes is caused by a virus similar to the one that causes cold sores, but here sores occur on the genitals. The first attack may last about 2 weeks. If a second attack occurs it is less severe than the first. Later attacks, which are less severe still, may be brought on by other illnesses or stress. There is no cure, but an antiviral ointment can be used to make the condition more comfortable.

AIDS or Acquired Immune Deficiency Syndrome is caused by the Human Immunodeficiency Virus or HIV. This virus attacks the lymphocytes (see page 64) and reduces the protective power of the immune system. A person who becomes infected with HIV may not develop any symptoms for a few years. During this time he/she could pass the virus on to others during sexual intercourse. HIV can also be passed on through infected blood. If this enters the blood of another person, that person may become infected. The virus can be passed on by infected drug addicts sharing needles with non-infected people. In the past some people who suffered from haemophilia became infected because the blood they were given as part of their treatment had not been checked for the virus. In the United Kingdom all blood used for haemophiliacs and for transfusions in operations is now checked to make sure that it is HIV-free. A person who thinks that he or she may have become infected with the HIV virus can have a test.

When the immune system is weakened by the HIV virus the body is open to attack by other disease-causing microbes and AIDS develops. There is loss of weight, tiredness, and there may be the development of a type of skin cancer. Death eventually occurs, often through pneumonia. There is no cure for AIDS at the moment.

1 How does the health of a person infected with **a)** gonorrhoea and **b)** syphilis deteriorate without treatment?
2 If a person was told that they were HIV-negative after a test for HIV what do you think this means?
3 What would they be told if the test showed that they had become infected with the HIV virus?
4 Why do you think people are offered counselling before they take an HIV test and before they are given the results?
5 What causes the death of many AIDS sufferers?

Figure A Counselling helps many people to cope when they learn they have the HIV virus.

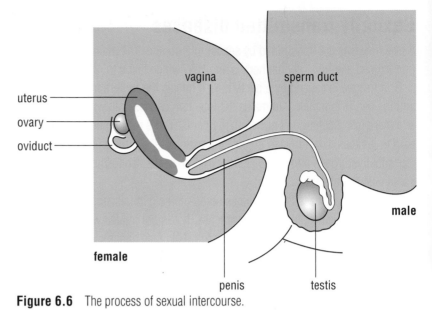

Figure 6.6 The process of sexual intercourse.

Path of the sperm

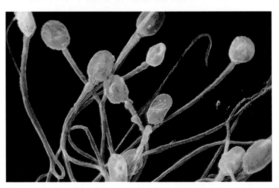

Figure 6.7 Photomicrograph of sperm cells.

The semen ejaculated into the top of the vagina contains over 400 million sperm. The sperm cells do not contain a food store to provide them with energy for movement. They get their nourishment from the seminal fluid which was secreted by glands as the sperm made their way from the testicles to the urethra. The food provides each sperm with energy to lash its tail like a whip. This movement drives the sperm forwards.

The sperm travel through the cervix and up the mucus lining of the uterus wall into the oviducts. It takes them 4–6 hours to make their journey. Millions die on the way leaving only a few thousand to enter the oviduct. As the sperm swim along the oviduct even more die so that only a few hundred reach their destination. The sperm may survive for 2 or 3 days here before they die. During this time, if the sperm meet an egg, fertilisation may occur.

9 Compare the ways in which the sperm and egg move along the oviduct.

How the egg is moved

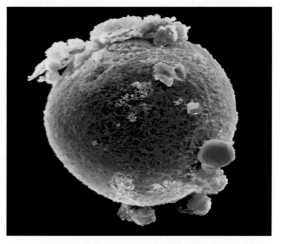

Figure 6.8 Photomicrograph of an egg.

The egg is much larger than a sperm cell because it contains its own food store. This is to provide energy and materials for the very early development of the embryo if the egg is fertilised. Unlike the sperm, the egg has no means of propulsion. It is moved by the action of the cilia in the wall of the oviduct. They wave backwards and forwards and push the egg along.

Fertilisation

When the sperm cells meet an egg in the oviduct they crowd around it. The head of only one sperm cell penetrates the cell membrane of the egg. This sperm cell's head breaks off from the tail and moves through the egg cell's cytoplasm to the nucleus. When the head

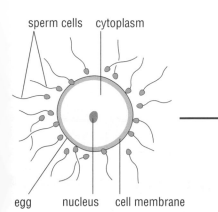

sperm cells   cytoplasm

egg   nucleus   cell membrane

path of sperm head
inside the egg

fertilisation to
form a zygote

Figure 6.9 Fertilisation.

reaches the egg cell's nucleus fertilisation takes place. In this process the nucleus inside the sperm head fuses with the egg cell nucleus. The fertilised egg is called a zygote. Changes to the cell membrane around the zygote prevent other sperm heads from entering and fusing with the nucleus.

If the fertilised egg becomes implanted into the uterus wall conception has taken place. It results in pregnancy. As long as there are no problems, a mother remains pregnant until birth takes place.

IVF

IVF stands for '*in vitro* fertilisation' which means 'in glass fertilisation'. It results in what has been termed a 'test-tube baby'. The IVF process is used to help couples who produce sperm and eggs but fertilisation will not take place in the oviduct. The treatment may follow this plan. The woman is given a fertility drug to increase egg maturation in the ovaries. A technique known as laparoscopy is used to remove the eggs from the ovary. In this operation a small cut is made in the side of the woman's abdomen and a fibre-optic tube is inserted into the body so that the surgeon can see the ovary and remove the eggs.

1 Why do you think it is a good idea to collect more than one egg at one time?

For discussion

Some people do not believe that a frozen embryo should be treated as a person. Do you think they are correct?

These people believe that unwanted frozen embryos should be destroyed. Do you agree? Explain your answer.

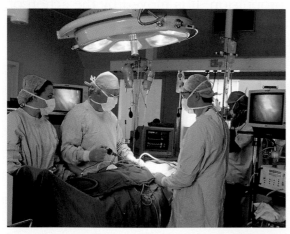

Figure A   Laparoscopy operation.

The man then provides the sperm and they are mixed with the eggs in a glass dish. The eggs are checked under the microscope to see if fertilisation has taken place. Then, one or two fertilised eggs are placed in the woman's uterus and the others are stored by freezing them in liquid nitrogen. These stored embryos can be used later if the first ones fail to develop or if the couple want more children.

Figure B   Human embryo storage.

Development of the baby

After fertilisation the zygote divides into two cells, then four, then eight and so on. The zygote does not increase in size, so cells become smaller at each division. By 7 days after fertilisation the cells have formed a hollow ball and have reached the uterus. The hollow ball sinks into the thick lining of the uterus wall, which has a large amount of blood passing through it. This process of sinking into the uterus wall is called implantation.

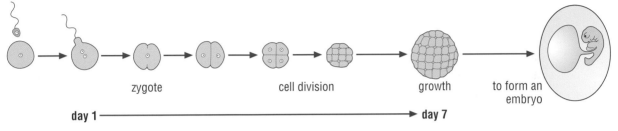

zygote   cell division   growth   to form an embryo

day 1 ———————————————————→ day 7

Figure 6.10 The early development of the zygote into an embryo.

Twins

About one in a hundred pregnancies produces twins. The twins may be identical or non-identical. Identical twins form from the same fertilised egg. At the first cell division of the zygote the two cells move apart and each one develops into an embryo. Non-identical twins form from two eggs that are released into the oviduct at the same time. Each egg is fertilised by a different sperm. Identical twins share the same genetic material (see page 154) but non-identical twins have different genetic material.

In some very rare circumstances, conjoined (popularly called Siamese) twins develop. They are identical twins but the cells from which they formed did not separate completely. They may be joined at the head, the hip or the chest. They may have two sets of organs or one twin may be without one or more organs and rely on the other for survival.

1 A boy and girl are a pair of twins. Are they identical or non-identical? Explain your answer.
2 What could be the consequence of separating conjoined twins who share some organs? Explain your answer.

Figure A

Identical twins

Non-identical twins

Placenta

The cells on the surface of the hollow ball of cells of the zygote will form the placenta. This takes in food and oxygen from the mother's blood so that the cells can grow and divide. Waste products, such as carbon dioxide from the cells' activities, pass across the placenta to the mother's blood so she can remove them through her own lungs or kidneys.

During the course of the pregnancy the placenta grows into a disc with a diameter of about 20 cm. It forms microscopic finger-like projections called villi that penetrate into the uterus wall and make a very large surface area for the exchange of materials between the mother and her baby. The placenta is attached to the developing baby by the umbilical cord. Blood runs through vessels in this cord between the placenta and the baby's tissues. The baby's blood and the mother's blood always remain separate. The mother's blood is at a much higher pressure than the baby's blood so it would damage its blood vessels if it passed directly through the placenta. The two kinds of blood may not be compatible. This means that if they mixed, clotting would occur which would block the blood vessels and lead to further damage.

The placenta makes hormones that stop the ovaries producing any more eggs and keep the uterus wall from breaking down as it would normally do in the menstrual cycle (see page 83). Antibodies pass from the mother's blood through the placenta to her baby to give protection from diseases.

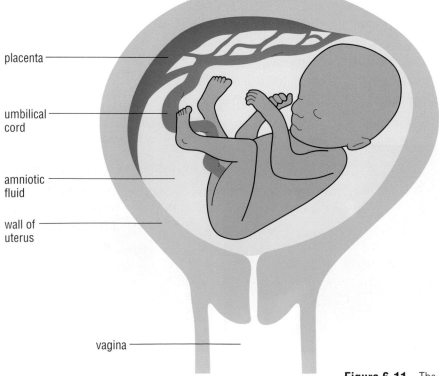

placenta

umbilical cord

amniotic fluid

wall of uterus

vagina

Figure 6.11 The fetus in the uterus.

Embryo and fetus

Although most people refer to a baby growing in the uterus, the words embryo and fetus are often used for the early stages. While some of the cells inside the hollow ball join with those on the outside to make the placenta, most of the cells form the embryo. At the end of the first 2 weeks of development the embryo is a flat disc of tissue, but by 4 weeks it has developed a simple body shape with stumps where the limbs will grow. Internally its heart has started to beat. By 8 weeks all of the organ systems have formed and the embryo, which is now 2.5 cm long, is called a fetus.

The fetus continues to increase in size and the organ systems become more fully developed. By 14 weeks the sex of the fetus can be revealed by an ultrasound scan and at about 16 weeks the fetus makes movements that the mother can feel. The head and body of the fetus at this time is only about 10 cm. By 20 weeks the fetus is 12.5 cm long but its legs are growing quickly. Eight weeks later the fetus turns upside down with its head towards the cervix. The alveoli in its lungs begin to grow at this stage and continue to grow after the birth. Before birth the lungs contain a fluid. They do not expand until just after the baby is born. At the end of 38 weeks after fertilisation of the egg the fetus is about 50 cm long and has a mass of about 3 kg.

The baby is now ready to be born. The length of time between fertilisation and birth is called the gestation period. In medicine this is referred to as 40 weeks (rather than 38 weeks) because the time is calculated from the first day of the last menstrual period.

Amnion and its fluid

During the development of the fetus a bag called the amnion containing watery fluid forms around it. The fluid acts like a cushion around the fetus and protects it from pressures outside the uterus that might squash it. The mother, for example, may be accidentally pushed against in a crowded street. The fluid also allows the fetus to float freely so that growing limbs have space to develop and are not pressed against the wall of the uterus where their growth would be restricted.

10 How do the placenta and the amniotic fluid help the embryo and fetus develop?

11 How is an embryo different from a fetus?

12 How is the fetus put at risk if the mother smokes and drinks alcohol while she is pregnant?

Damaging the fetus

If the mother smokes during her pregnancy the amount of oxygen reaching the fetus is reduced. This may hinder the baby's development and might result in the baby's mass being 200 g below normal when it is born.

Drinking alcohol regularly during pregnancy increases the risk of miscarriage. This occurs when the placenta detaches from the uterus wall and the fetus dies. Drinking alcohol also increases the chance of the newborn baby being less well developed mentally and physically.

Drugs such as LSD and amphetamines contain poisons that affect the healthy development of the fetus. If the mother is a heroin addict the baby will also be addicted.

Miscarriage and abortion

A miscarriage occurs when the placenta naturally comes away from the uterus wall. It may be due to the death of the fetus, some abnormality in its development or a defect in the placenta. It is sometimes known as a spontaneous abortion.

An induced abortion is the removal of the fetus. An abortion may be performed if it is thought that the pregnancy is putting the mother's health or life at risk. It may also be performed if tests show that the fetus is developing very abnormally and would suffer from severe mental or physical handicap or both. Abortion may in some cases be used to end an unwanted pregnancy even though the lives of the mother or the fetus are not at risk. In the United Kingdom it is illegal for an abortion to take place after 24 weeks of pregnancy because after that time the fetus can live independently outside the womb.

1 What are the differences between a miscarriage and an induced abortion?

2 When could an abortion be justified?

Birth

There are three stages to the birth process. In the first stage the muscles in the uterus wall begin to contract. The time between each contraction may be up to 30 minutes at first. During the 12 to 14 hours of this first stage the time between contractions shortens to 2 to 3 minutes. At some point the contractions cause the amnion to break and the fluid to pass out down the vagina. This is called the 'breaking of the waters'. At the end of the first stage the cervix has widened so that the head of the fetus can start to pass down it.

In the second stage the mother contracts her abdominal muscles with the contractions of the uterus to push the fetus down the birth canal. This stage may only last a few minutes and is completed when the baby has been born and the umbilical cord has been cut and clamped to prevent loss of blood. If there are twins the contractions stop for about 10 minutes after the first baby has been born then start again. Only a few contractions may be needed for the second baby to be born.

The two stages from the first contractions of the uterus to the birth of the baby is called labour.

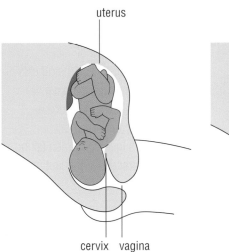
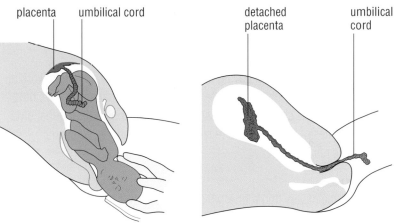

uterus

cervix   vagina

placenta   umbilical cord

detached placenta

umbilical cord

Figure 6.12   Diagrammatic representation of birth.

The third stage lasts for about 20 minutes after the second. During this time the placenta comes away from the wall of the uterus and passes down the vagina. When it has left the mother the placenta is called the afterbirth.

Premature babies

Labour may occur earlier than normal for several reasons, such as the mother being ill or the uterus not being correctly formed. A baby is premature if it is born after the 23rd week of pregnancy and before the 37th week. A premature baby will have a lower weight than normal and poorly developed lungs. It may be placed in an incubator where it is kept warm, given extra oxygen to breathe and fed through a tube in the nose. Hospitals also have wards for premature babies called neonatal intensive care units. Most premature babies survive their early birth.

1 How has the use of an incubator improved a premature baby's chances of survival?

Figure A   Premature baby in an incubator.

Contraception

It is possible for a couple to have a child every year until the woman starts the menopause (see page 83). A very large family would soon be produced which would be difficult for most people to afford. In all communities most couples practise some form of contraceptive method of birth control or family planning to prevent unwanted pregnancies. The methods of contraception are divided into three groups.

1 Preventing sperm from reaching the egg

Rhythm method

This method depends on studying the female's menstrual cycle and working out when the egg is most likely to be in the oviduct. When these days have been identified the couple avoid having sexual intercourse during that time but other times of the month are regarded as 'safe periods' for sexual intercourse to take place.

Condom

This is a tube of very thin rubber which is placed over the erect penis before sexual intercourse. The semen collects at the tip of the condom after ejaculation.

Cap

This is a dome-shaped piece of rubber that is inserted at the top of the vagina by the female before sexual intercourse takes place. It stops the sperm going through the cervix.

Spermicides

These are chemicals in a foam or a cream that kill sperm. They are less efficient if they are used on their own on the penis and in the vagina and are usually used with the cap or condom for extra prevention against sperm reaching an egg.

Vasectomy

The sperm duct is cut and tied off to prevent the sperm reaching the urethra. The glands that make the seminal fluid still produce secretions that can be ejaculated. A vasectomy is an operation that usually cannot be reversed.

Female sterilisation

The oviducts are cut and tied off. Eggs continue to be released from the ovaries but they cannot reach the uterus. This operation usually cannot be reversed.

1 Which methods of contraception involve surgery?
2 Which methods may be suitable for a couple who definitely do not want any more children? Explain your answer.
3 How is stopping implantation a different method of contraception from the others?
4 Identify the contraceptive devices shown in Figure A.
5 Why do you think most methods involve women taking the contraceptive precaution?

(continued)

2 Stopping the ovaries from making eggs

The contraceptive pill is taken daily for 3 weeks of the menstrual cycle. The pills contain one or more female sex hormones that stop the ovaries releasing an egg. After menstruation has taken place another 3 week course of pills is taken. Some women find the pill has side-effects that make them feel unwell.

3 Stopping implantation

Implantation occurs when the ball of cells produced after fertilisation sinks into the wall of the uterus and becomes connected to it. A plastic coil, called an Intra Uterine Device or IUD, is placed in the uterus by a doctor. When the ball of cells reaches the uterus it is stopped from implanting and the cells die.

Some of these methods are more reliable at preventing conception than others. For example, the menstrual cycle may be earlier or later than usual, depending on the health of the female. This change in the menstrual cycle makes it more difficult to judge the time of the safe period used in the rhythm method. In comparison, the condom and the contraceptive pill are more reliable methods of contraception because the condom forms a barrier that prevents the sperm reaching the egg, and the contraceptive pill prevents an egg from reaching the oviduct where fertilisation could take place.

A couple may choose a method of contraception for religious or moral reasons. For example, they may feel that there should not be any kind of unnatural way of preventing a sperm meeting an egg and therefore choose the rhythm method. The IUD may not be used because a couple might believe that when a ball of cells forms it is a person and preventing it implanting is the same as not allowing a person to live.

Figure A A selection of contraceptive devices.

Early life

The baby starts to suck as soon as it is born. During pregnancy some of the hormones produced by the mother cause the milk-secreting or mammary glands in her breasts to develop. The milk that the mother provides for her baby contains all the nutrients the baby needs. It also contains antibodies to protect the baby from disease. Some mothers cannot provide enough milk for their babies and use special powdered milk made up into a liquid instead. This is delivered in a sterile bottle and teat.

The end of the umbilical cord attached to the baby withers away and falls off leaving the navel.

The baby continues to grow rapidly and the organ systems become more co-ordinated. At the end of the first month the baby can hold its head up for a few seconds. In the following months the baby can lift its head more steadily, kick and push itself up on its hands. It will listen and look for the sources of sounds by moving its eyes and turning its head and respond by making cooing and gurgling sounds of its own.

Figure 6.12 Young children need a stimulating environment in which to grow up.

13 How does the body of a person change from the moment just before they are born to the time just before puberty?

By 6 months the baby's first set of teeth start to push through its gums. The baby's diet is gradually changed to solid foods. When this happens, usually before 12 months, the baby is said to be weaned. All parts of the body continue to grow but at about 4 years of age the head has reached almost its full size. The sex organs do not develop fully until puberty.

◆ SUMMARY ◆

◆ Changes in the body at puberty are brought about by the sex hormones (*see page 79*).

◆ The male and female reproductive organs have differences and similarities (*see pages 81 and 82*).

◆ The menstrual cycle occurs due to the monthly release of an egg (*see page 83*).

◆ Some diseases are transmitted by sexual intercourse (*see page 85*).

◆ Fertilisation is the fusion of a sperm nucleus with an egg nucleus (*see page 87*).

◆ Development of the embryo takes place in the uterus (*see page 89*).

◆ Twins may be identical or non-identical (*see page 89*).

◆ The placenta and the amnion play important parts in the development of the embryo and fetus (*see pages 90 and 91*).

◆ The fetus may be lost by miscarriage or abortion (*see page 92*).

◆ The uterus and abdominal muscles are used in the birth process (*see page 92*).

◆ Contraception prevents unwanted pregnancies (*see pages 94–95*).

◆ Many body changes take place in the child's early life (*see page 96*).

End of chapter question

1 How does a knowledge of the basic facts of reproduction help someone going through puberty?

For discussion

'People should develop a responsible attitude towards sex.' What do you think this means?

7 | *How green plants live*

How experiments build up information

Scientific processes are not usually understood by a single activity or even one repeated several times for checking. Processes are worked out over many years by a large number of different experiments that require different apparatus and different techniques and may include making observations, thinking up new ideas and making models to test ideas. The activities form part of a line of research that may go back many years. The results of each experiment may contribute something to our understanding of how a process works. Eventually the results of a large number of different activities may show how the process works. In the following pages a series of experiments are presented as very simple examples of how their results contributed to our understanding of how plants make food.

If you become a scientist you will use some of the features you read here, such as looking at the work of others or learning a technique to use in your experiments, in addition to making investigations following the scientific method.

The willow tree experiment

In the 17th Century Joannes Baptista van Helmont performed an experiment on a willow tree. He was interested in what made it grow. At that time scientists believed that everything was made from four 'elements': air, water, fire and earth. Van Helmont believed that water was the most basic 'element' in the universe and that everything was made from it. He set up his experiment by weighing a willow sapling and the soil it was to grow in. Then he planted the sapling in the soil and provided it with nothing but water for the next 5 years. At the end of his experiment he found that the tree had increased in mass by 73 kilograms but the soil had decreased in mass by only about 60 grams. He concluded that the increase in mass was due to the water the plant had received.

1 How fair was van Helmont's experiment? Explain your answer.

2 Did the result of the experiment support van Helmont's beliefs? Explain your answer.

3 If you were to repeat van Helmont's experiment how would you improve it and what table would you construct for recording your results?

Figure 7.1 Watering a willow tree.

If we were to summarise his conclusion it could look like this:

$$water \rightarrow mass\ of\ plant$$

Revising the work so far

As plants are food for animals the simple equation could be rewritten as:

$$water \rightarrow food\ in\ the\ plant$$

Moving on

The idea of food in the plant could then be investigated. A reasonable place to start could be with a plant part that is used as food – the potato.

Examining a potato with a microscope

If a small slice of potato is examined under the microscope the cells are found to contain colourless grains. When dilute iodine solution is added to the potato slice the grains turn blue–black. This test shows that the grains are made of starch.

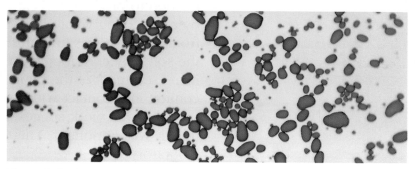

Figure 7.2 Starch grains.

Moving on

Having established that plant tubers such as the potato contain starch it may then be reasonable to try and find out if other parts of the plant contain starch. As the leaves are a major feature of most plants the search for starch in leaves would be the next task.

Testing a leaf for starch

Iodine does not produce a colour change when it is placed on a leaf because the cell walls will not allow the iodine into the cells and the green pigment masks any colour change. However, the work of others has shown that a leaf can be tested for starch if it is first treated with boiling water and ethanol. The boiling water makes it easier for liquids to leave and enter the plant cells and the ethanol removes the green pigment, chlorophyll, from the leaf and makes the leaf crisp.

If the leaves of a geranium that has been growing on a windowsill or in a greenhouse are tested, they will be found to contain starch.

4 What was the purpose of putting the leaf **a)** in boiling water and **b)** in ethanol?

Revising the work so far

Starch belongs to a nutrient group called carbohydrates, so, perhaps the simple equation could be altered to:

$$\text{water} \rightarrow \text{carbohydrate (starch) in the plant}$$

Moving on

Stephen Hales (1677–1761) discovered that 'a portion of air' helped a plant to survive and Jan Ingenhousz (1730–1799) showed that green plants take up carbon dioxide from the air when they are put in the light. It was also known that water only contains the elements hydrogen and oxygen while carbohydrates contain carbon, hydrogen and oxygen. All this information led to a review of van Helmont's idea that only water was needed to produce the carbohydrate. The review began by considering what else was around the plant apart from water. It was known from van Helmont's work that the soil only contributed a very small amount to the increased mass of the plant. The only other material coming into contact with the plant was the air. Ingenhousz's work suggested that the carbon dioxide in the air was important. This idea can be tested in the laboratory.

Destarching a plant

If you want to see whether starch has been made you have to start with a plant that does not have starch. If a plant that has leaves containing starch is left in darkness for 2 or 3 days then tested again it will be found that the leaves are starch-free. The plant is described as a destarched plant. It can be used to test for the effect of carbon dioxide.

Investigating the effect of carbon dioxide on starch production

Soda lime is a substance that absorbs carbon dioxide and takes it out of the air. Sodium hydrogencarbonate solution is a liquid that releases carbon dioxide into the air.

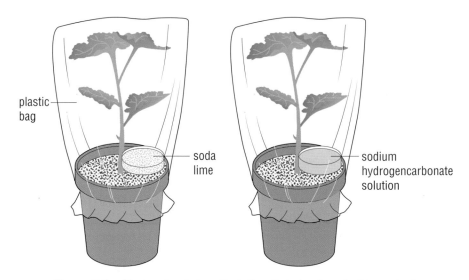

Figure 7.3 Plants set up to investigate the effect of carbon dioxide on starch production.

Two destarched plants were set up under transparent plastic bags that were sealed with an elastic band. Before covering the plants with the bags, a small dish of soda lime was added to one plant and a small dish of sodium hydrogencarbonate solution was added to the other. Both plants were left in daylight for a few hours before a leaf from each of them was tested for starch.

The leaf from the plant with the soda lime dish did not contain starch but the leaf from the plant with the sodium hydrogencarbonate did contain starch. This suggested that carbon dioxide is needed for starch production.

5 What does soda lime do to the air inside the plastic bag?
6 What does sodium hydrogencarbonate do to the air inside the plastic bag?

Revising the work so far

After reviewing the result of the effect of carbon dioxide on starch production the simple equation can be modified again to:

carbon dioxide + water → carbohydrate (starch) in a plant

Moving on

Joseph Priestley (1733–1804) studied how things burn. At that time scientists used the phlogiston theory to explain how things burned. They believed that when materials such as wood burned they lost a substance called phlogiston. When a candle burned in a closed volume of air, such as the air in a bell jar, they believed that the candle eventually went out because the air had become filled with phlogiston. It had become phlogisticated.

When Priestley put a plant in the air in which a candle had burned he found that later on a candle would burn in it again. He reasoned that the plant had taken the phlogiston out of the air and had made dephlogisticated air. Later, Ingenhouz re-examined Priestley's results and found that the phlogiston theory was wrong. The plants had in fact produced oxygen.

Water plants can be used to investigate the gases produced by plants because the gases escape from their surface in bubbles that can be easily seen and collected.

Investigating oxygen production in plants

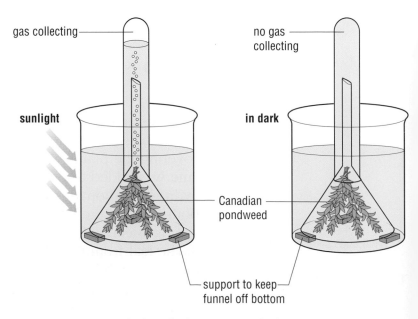

Figure 7.4 Apparatus for investigating oxygen production.

Two samples of Canadian pondweed were set up as shown in Figure 7.4. One was put in a sunny place and the other was kept in the dark. After about a week the amount of gas collected in each test-tube was examined. The plants in the dark had not produced any gas. The plants in the light had produced gas and when it was tested with a glowing splint the splint relighted showing that the gas contained more oxygen than normal air.

Revising the work so far

From the result of this experiment the equation can be further modified to:

$$\text{carbon dioxide} + \text{water} \rightarrow \text{carbohydrate} + \text{oxygen}$$

Moving on

Having established that the carbohydrate starch is formed in leaves it may seem reasonable to find out what affects the presence of starch in leaves. What is it in the plant that allows the reaction to happen? Does the reaction happen all the time or only at certain times of the day or night?

Testing the effect of light on a destarched plant

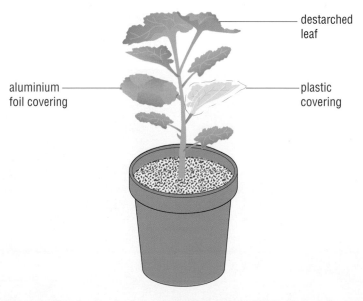

Figure 7.5 Two leaves of a destarched plant covered with plastic and aluminium.

Two leaves of a destarched plant were set up as shown in Figure 7.5 and left for over 4 hours in daylight. After that time they were removed and tested for the presence of starch. The leaf kept in the transparent plastic sheet contained starch. The leaf kept in the aluminium sheet did not contain any starch. This suggested that light is needed for starch to form in a leaf.

Revising the work so far

After reviewing the result of the effect of light on the leaf the equation can be modified to:

$$\text{carbon dioxide} + \text{water} \xrightarrow{\text{light}} \text{carbohydrate} + \text{oxygen}$$

Light provides the energy for the chemical reaction to take place. Some of the energy is stored as chemical energy in the carbohydrate.

Moving on

Having discovered a connection between the leaf, light and starch production it may seem reasonable to find out which part of the leaf is important. As most leaves are green it may be suggested that the green pigment, chlorophyll, which is found in chloroplasts of the leaf, is important. If it is lacking, starch should not be made. This hypothesis can be tested by using a variegated leaf, which has some cells that do not have chlorophyll thus making parts of the leaf appear white.

Investigating chlorophyll and starch production

A destarched variegated plant was left in daylight for over 4 hours. A leaf was then removed and tested for starch. The parts that were green contained starch but the parts that were white did not contain starch. This suggested that chlorophyll is needed for the leaf to produce starch.

Figure 7.6 A variegated pelargonium called Lady Plymouth.

Revising the work so far

After reviewing the result of the effect of chlorophyll on starch production, the equation can be modified to:

$$\text{carbon dioxide} + \text{water} \xrightarrow[\text{chlorophyll}]{\text{light}} \text{carbohydrate} + \text{oxygen}$$

Further experiments showed that the carbohydrate starch was built up in stages from subunits of a substance called glucose. The equation for starch production, or photosynthesis, is now written as:

$$\text{carbon dioxide} + \text{water} \xrightarrow[\text{chlorophyll}]{\text{light}} \text{glucose} + \text{oxygen}$$

7 Try to describe photosynthesis in your own words.

Fate of glucose

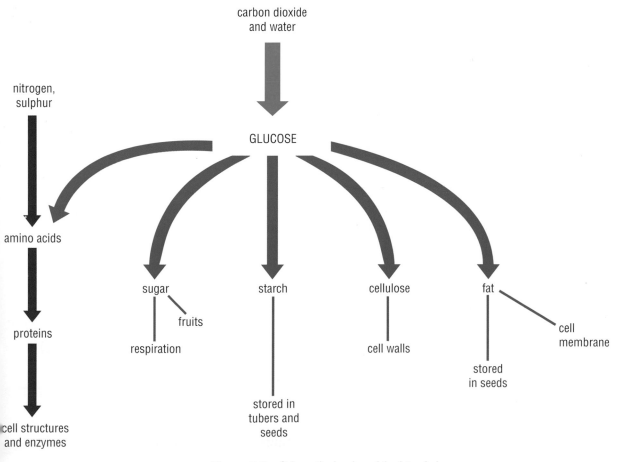

Figure 7.7 Schematic drawing of the fate of glucose.

Glucose may be used to release energy in the process of respiration. The energy released is used for all life processes in plant cells. Glucose is also used to make many other molecules in the plant. It may be used to make cellulose for the cell walls or turned into fats for the cell membranes. Glucose may be changed into starch, which is an energy store for the plant, or made into sugars in fruits so that their sweet taste makes them attractive to animals (see page 124). Nitrogen and sulphur join with the elements in glucose to make amino acids and proteins.

Plant respiration

Plant cells need energy to drive their life processes. As in animals, this energy is released in respiration (see page 42):

glucose + oxygen → carbon dioxide + water + energy

Plants respire 24 hours a day. They take in oxygen and produce carbon dioxide. During daylight photosynthesis also takes place. In this reaction carbon dioxide is used up and oxygen is produced. In bright sunlight the speed at which plants produce oxygen is greater than the speed at which they use up oxygen in respiration.

Glucose and starch

Glucose is soluble in the cell sap. If the concentration of glucose in the cell sap is too high too much water is drawn into the cell. When glucose is made in large quantities in the leaf cells it is converted into starch, which is insoluble and does not affect the way water enters or leaves the plant cells. When the concentration of glucose in the cell becomes low the starch is converted back into glucose.

Oxygen and carbon dioxide in the atmosphere

About 20% of the atmosphere is composed of oxygen and about 0.03% is composed of carbon dioxide. These two amounts remain the same from year to year. The reason they do not change is that the carbon dioxide produced by animals and plants in respiration is used up in photosynthesis, and the oxygen produced by the plants is used up by plants and animals in respiration.

8 What do plants take from the air and give to the air when they respire?

9 What do plants take from the air and give to the air during photosynthesis?

10 Compare the equations for photosynthesis and respiration.

11 How does the amount of
a) carbon dioxide and
b) oxygen vary around a plant over a 24-hour period? Explain your answer.

12 When will the amount of glucose in a leaf cell rise to a high concentration? Explain your answer.

13 Why does starch form?

14 When will the amount of starch in a leaf cell decrease? Explain why this happens.

15 Why do humans not suffocate at night when the plants around them cannot photosynthesise?

16 What effect will reducing the number of plants on the surface of our planet have on the animals?

Figure 7.8 Some of the oxygen that these deer are breathing has been produced by the trees around them.

Carbon cycle

The carbon dioxide taken into a plant is used to make glucose, which may be transported to a storage organ and converted into starch. If the storage organ is a potato, for example, it may be dug up out of the ground, cooked and eaten. The starch is broken down in digestion to glucose and taken into the blood. In the body the glucose may be used for respiration and the carbon is released as carbon dioxide. If too much high energy food is being eaten the glucose may be converted into fat and the carbon remains in the body. When the body dies, microbes feed on it and break it down into simple substances. The microbes thus release the carbon back into the air, as carbon dioxide, when they respire.

17 Re-read the account of the carbon cycle and draw the paths that carbon can take.

18 Now add in the path that the carbon would take if the potato plant died.

19 Why is the path called the carbon cycle?

Plants and planets

The first plants were algae. They lived in the sea. Today, huge numbers of algae live in the plankton. This is the name given to the algae and tiny animals that live in the upper waters of the oceans. Most of the oxygen you breathe has been produced by algae.

About 400 million years ago, when the oxygen concentration of the atmosphere was about 1%, the first land plants developed. They were similar to horsetails (see page 141) and had relatively simple structures. Later, mosses, ferns and conifers developed. The first flowering plants developed 170 million years ago.

Humans developed in the last 2 million years and originally hunted animals for food or collected berries and roots to eat.

About 10 000 years ago humans discovered that more food could be obtained by planting seeds in the soil to grow crops. Today, the main food crops are wheat, barley, maize, millet, sorghum, rice, yams, plantain, cassava and potato. The main growing regions for these crops are shown in Figure A overleaf.

1 Which of the main food crops do you eat regularly?

2 Make a list of everything you eat for 2 days. Now remove all these main food crops and their products, such as popcorn (from maize), from your list.
   a) What foods would now remain in your diet?
   b) How important are these food crops to your diet? Explain your answer.

(continued)

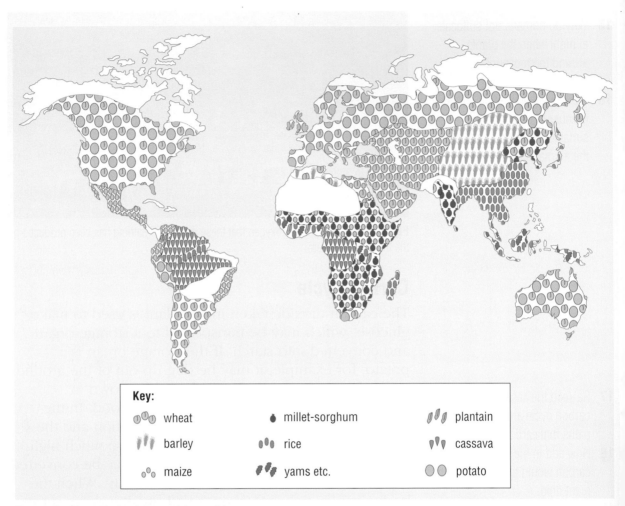

Key:

wheat		millet-sorghum		plantain	
barley		rice		cassava	
maize		yams etc.		potato	

Figure A   The main food crops of the world.

Figure B   Reclaiming the desert.

In many places the natural vegetation has been destroyed to make room for people and farms, but in deserts plants are being used to develop small areas of land.

It has been suggested that if we wish to colonise another planet in the future, we may need to send specially developed plants there to spread across its surface in order to change the atmosphere into a breathable one.

20 Put the information about mineral salts and their uses by plants into a table. Include information about what happens if the mineral salt is missing.

21 What mineral might be missing if the leaves go yellow?

22 Why might a plant show poor growth?

Mineral salts

When chemists began studying plants they discovered that they contained a wide range of elements. With the exceptions of carbon, hydrogen and oxygen the plants obtained these elements from mineral salts in the soil.

The importance of each element was assessed by setting up experiments in which the plants received all the necessary mineral salts except for the one under investigation. From these studies it was found that:

- nitrogen is taken in as nitrates and is needed to form proteins and chlorophyll. Without nitrogen the plant's leaves turn yellow and the plant shows poor growth.
- phosphorus is taken in as phosphates and is needed to make chemicals for the transfer of energy in photosynthesis and respiration. Without phosphorus a plant shows poor·growth.
- potassium is taken in in potassium salt and helps the plant to make protein and chlorophyll. If it is lacking the leaves become yellow and grow abnormally.

Lack of nitrogen

Lack of phosphorus

Lack of potassium

Figure 7.9 Plants showing mineral deficiency.

Path of minerals through living things

When animals eat plants they take in the minerals and use them in their bodies. Some of the minerals are released in the solid and liquid wastes that animals produce. As bacteria feed on these wastes, the mineral salts are released back into the soil. The mineral salts are also released when the plants and animals die and microbes break down their bodies in the process of

23 Could you be a recycled dinosaur? Explain your answer.

feeding. Plants, animals and their wastes are biodegradable. This means they can be broken down into simple substances that can be used again to make new living organisms. These simple substances have been recycled since the beginning of life on Earth.

Water and minerals in the plant

Most plant roots have projections called root hairs. The tips of the root hairs grow out into the spaces between the soil particles. There may be up to 500 root hairs in a square centimetre of root surface. They greatly increase the surface area of the root so that large quantities of water can pass through them into the plant. The water in the soil is drawn into the plant to replace the water that is lost through evaporation from the leaves. The plant does not have to use energy to take the water in.

Mineral salts are dissolved in the soil water. The plant has to use energy to take them in. This energy is provided by the root cells when they use oxygen in respiration. The roots get the oxygen from the air spaces between the soil particles.

24 If a plant is over-watered all the spaces between the soil particles become filled with water. How does this water-logged soil affect **a)** the plant roots and **b)** the plant's growth?

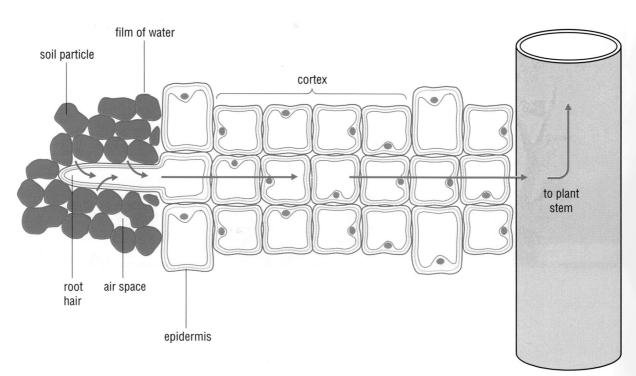

Figure 7.10   Schematic drawing of the movement of water and mineral salts in the root of a plant.

Carnivorous plants

Some plants live in conditions where minerals are unavailable. They are therefore unable to take up minerals from the soil. These plants have developed a way of getting the elements they need. Their leaves have adapted to allow them to trap and kill animals. The most important element required is nitrogen.

Butterwort and sundew grow in peaty bogs in the United Kingdom. The Venus fly trap grows in peaty bogs and waterlogged ground in the south-east of the United States. Pitcher plants (see Figure B) are found in tropical rainforests, in marshes in the United States and in some swamps in Australia. Bladderwort (see Figure B) is found in ponds in the United Kingdom.

The butterwort has leaves arranged in a rosette around the flower stalks. Each leaf is from 2 to 8 cm long. On the upper surface of the leaf are hairs that secrete a liquid containing protein-digesting enzymes. The edges of the leaf turn up to make a lip that prevents the sticky liquid from flowing away into the soil. If an insect lands on the liquid it cannot escape. Its soft parts are digested and absorbed into the leaf.

The leaves of the sundew have long stalks and circular blades. The upper surface of the leaf blade is covered in hairs that secrete sticky drops of a liquid that contains protein-digesting enzymes. When an insect lands on the leaf it sticks to the hairs and the enzymes digest its soft parts, leaving the hard parts to be blown away by the wind.

Each leaf of the Venus fly trap is divided into two halves that can spring together in 0.03 seconds. There are three hairs on each half of the leaf which act as triggers. If an insect lands on the leaf and touches them the trap is sprung. The spines on the edges of the leaf interlock and stop the insect escaping. A liquid is secreted from the leaf's surface which digests and absorbs the insect's body. In 24 hours the leaf opens again. After it has digested four insects the leaf dies and is replaced by a new one.

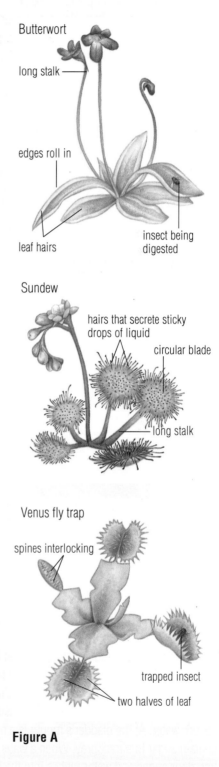

Butterwort
long stalk
edges roll in
leaf hairs
insect being digested

Sundew
hairs that secrete sticky drops of liquid
circular blade
long stalk

Venus fly trap
spines interlocking
trapped insect
two halves of leaf

Figure A

(continued)

The rainforest pitcher plants are able to climb trees because they have cords, called tendrils, that stick out of their leaves. They curl around twigs and branches and give the pitcher plant support. The end of a tendril forms a hollow tube with a lid. This tube is called a pitcher and when it is fully grown the lid opens and water collects in it. The largest pitchers can hold up to 2 litres of water. There are glands at the mouth of the pitcher which produce nectar to attract insects. The inside walls of the pitcher are very smooth so that the insect loses its grip and falls into the water. Some pitcher plants also produce a drug in their nectar which makes the insect lose co-ordination and fall into the pitcher. There are hairs on the pitcher walls that point downwards to prevent the insect escaping. The insect drowns. As its body decays it releases nutrients into the water. These are absorbed by the walls of the pitcher. The pitcher plants that grow in the United States secrete enzymes and acids to digest the insects. In the Australian species, enzymes and bacteria break down the insects' bodies.

1　What kind of conditions do not provide enough minerals for plants to grow well?
2　Why is nitrogen particularly important for plant growth?
3　How successful are the plant traps? Explain your answer.
4　What methods are used by carnivorous plants to break down an insect's body?

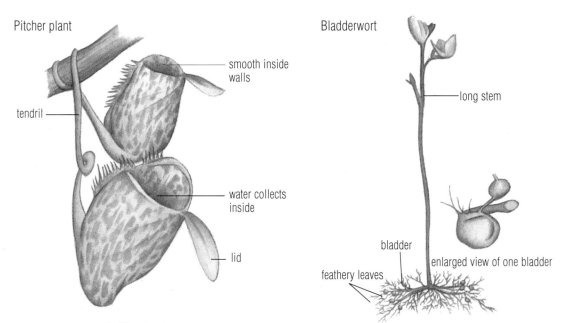

Figure B

The bladderwort is an aquatic plant that has pin-head sized traps on its feathery leaves. Each trap is called a bladder. The bladder is a globe-shaped structure that has a cavity which can be filled with water or air. The trap is set by removing the water from the cavity. Inside each bladder are cells that absorb water. At the bladder's mouth is a trap door, trigger hairs and cells that contain sugar to attract prey. When a water flea touches the trigger hairs the trap door opens and water rushes into the bladder carrying the water flea with it. The door closes behind it and the water flea is absorbed within a few days.

◆ SUMMARY ◆

- ◆ Iodine solution is used in the test for starch (*see page 99*).
- ◆ Boiling water and ethanol are used, with care, to remove chlorophyll from a leaf (*see page 100*).
- ◆ A plant is destarched by leaving it in the dark for 2 or 3 days (*see page 101*).
- ◆ Water and carbon dioxide are the raw materials of photosynthesis (*see page 102*).
- ◆ Light and chlorophyll are needed for a plant to photosynthesise (*see page 104*).
- ◆ Carbohydrate (glucose and starch) and oxygen are the products of photosynthesis (*see page 105*).
- ◆ Photosynthesis and respiration keep the levels of oxygen and carbon dioxide in the air constant (*see page 106*).
- ◆ Carbon passes from the air to a plant, then to an animal and finally a microbe releases it into the air again as it moves around the carbon cycle (*see page 107*).
- ◆ Mineral salts are needed for healthy plant growth (*see page 109*).
- ◆ Water and minerals enter the plant through the root hairs (*see page 110*).

End of chapter questions

How does a growing cucumber's weight change in a day? Large cucumbers appear to grow quickly. In this experiment a cucumber plant was placed close to a top-pan balance and one of its growing cucumbers was placed on the pan. The weight of the cucumber was measured every hour between 9.00 am and 4.00 pm. The weight was displayed in the graph in Figure 7.11.

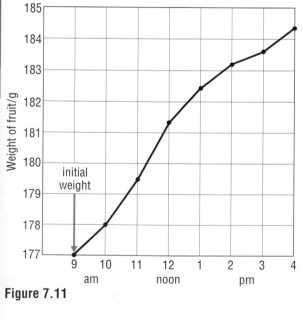

Figure 7.11

1 What was the gain in weight over the 7-hour period?

2 Construct a table to display the increase in weight in each of the 7 hours.

3 When was the period of **a)** greatest and **b)** least growth?

4 If the cucumber plant had some of its leaves removed before the experiment, how would you expect its growth graph to compare with the graph in this experiment? Explain your answer.

> For discussion
>
> Using only the information in this chapter suggest ways in which crop production could be improved.
>
> The rainforests have been described as the world's lungs. What do you think this means?

8 | Sexual reproduction in flowering plants

The male and female reproductive organs are found together in the flowers of most species of flowering plant. A flower forms at the tip of a stem on a part called the receptacle.

Parts of the flower

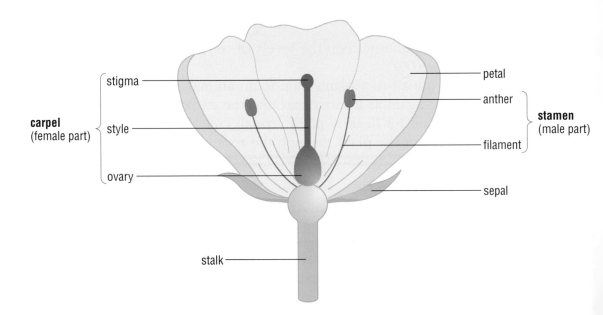

Figure 8.1 Parts of a typical insect-pollinated flower.

The outer part of the flower is formed by a ring of sepals called the calyx. Sepals are like small leaves and form a protective coat over the more delicate flower parts when the bud is developing.

Inside the sepals is a ring of petals called the corolla. The petals are usually large, brightly coloured parts of the flower.

Inside the ring of petals are the stamens which form the male part of the flower. Each stamen has two parts – the stalk, called the filament, and the pollen-producing organ, called the anther. The male gametes (see page 122) form inside the pollen grains.

Inside the ring of stamens is the female part of the flower which is made up from one or more carpels which may group together to from a pistil. Each carpel has a pollen-receiving surface called a stigma. Beneath the stigma is the style. It is connected to the ovary which contains one or more ovules. The female gametes form in the ovules.

1 What are the differences between a sepal and a petal?
2 In what ways are stamens and carpels **a)** different and **b)** similar?

Examples of flowers

The tulip has six petals, six stamens and six carpels.

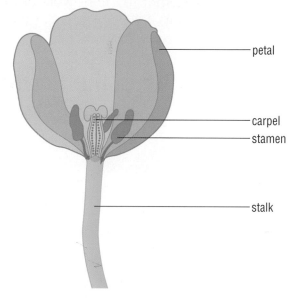

Figure 8.2   Inside a tulip.

The buttercup produces flowers from May to August. It has five sepals, five petals, up to 60 stamens and up to 40 carpels.

Figure 8.3   A buttercup.

The shepherd's purse can flower in every month of the year. It has small, white flowers that have four sepals, four petals, six stamens and a central pistil. The flowers are arranged in a group called an inflorescence.

Figure 8.4 Shepherd's purse.

The daisy and dandelion 'flowers' are made from a large number of smaller flowers, sometimes called florets. They form an inflorescence of tightly packed flowers which is called a flower head. The daisy has two kinds of floret in its flower head. The inner yellow florets have both male and female parts. The outer florets have a white strap which looks like a petal of the 'flower' and only has female parts. All the florets of the dandelion flower head have both male and female parts. There may be up to 300 of them on one flower head.

Figure 8.5 The florets of a dandelion flower head.

Pollen grains and pollination

When the pollen grains are fully formed in the anther it splits open to release them. Pollination occurs when pollen is transferred from an anther to a stigma. If the pollen goes from an anther to the stigma of the same flower or other flowers on the same plant the process is called self-pollination. Cross-pollination occurs if the pollen goes from the anther to the stigma of a flower on another plant of the same species. Most plants produce flowers that have both male and female reproductive parts. They avoid self-pollination in two ways. Firstly, the anther can release the pollen before the stigma is ready to receive it, or secondly, the stigmas can be ready to receive pollen from other plants of the same species before their own anthers are ready to release their pollen.

Self-pollination

Cross-pollination

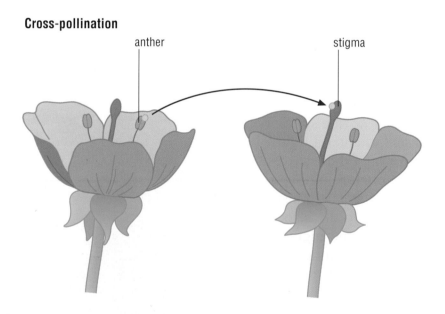

anther

stigma

Figure 8.6

There are two main ways in which the pollen grains are transferred from one flower to another for cross-pollination. They may be carried by insects or they may be carried by the wind. Pollen grains carried by insects may have a spiky surface which helps them stick to the hairs on the insect's body. Pollen grains carried by the wind are very small and light so that they can easily travel on air currents.

Insect and wind-pollinated flowers

The flowers of insect-pollinated plants are different from the flowers of wind-pollinated plants.

Insect-pollinated flowers have a range of adaptations that attract insects. These adaptations include large colourful petals, scent and nectaries that produce a sugary liquid called nectar on which the insects feed. Some flowers produce more pollen than is needed for pollination and this may be taken as food by the pollinating insect. Many insect-pollinated plants, such as orchids, are adapted so that they attract just one species of insect. The shape and arrangement of the petals may allow one species of insect to enter a flower but keep out other species. The structure of the flowers encourages the transfer of pollen onto the insect and then onto the stigma of a plant of the same species. Short filaments keep the anthers inside the flower so that the insect can brush past them. The anthers of insect-pollinated flowers make a smaller amount of pollen than those of wind-pollinated flowers. Their stigma is often flat and held on a short style inside the flower so that the insect can easily land on it.

Figure 8.7   Pollen from a wind-pollinated plant (top) and an insect-pollinated plant (bottom).

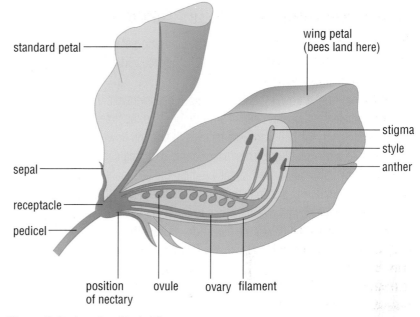

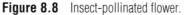

Figure 8.8 Insect-pollinated flower.

Wind-pollinated flowers are smaller than insect-pollinated flowers and do not show the adaptations shown above. They may have green petals that do not have nectar or scent. The flowers have long filaments which allow the anthers to sway outside the flower in the air currents. The anthers make a large amount of pollen and the stigma is a feathery structure which hangs outside the flower and forms a large surface area for catching pollen in the air.

3 Make a table to compare wind and insect-pollinated plants.
4 Why does one method of pollination require much more pollen than the other method?
5 What is the difference between self-pollination and cross-pollination?

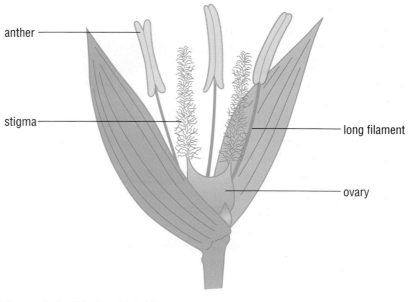

Figure 8.9 Wind-pollinated flower.

Bees and flowers

Karl von Frisch (1886–1982) was an Austrian zoologist who studied how bees communicate with each other. In 1973 he received a Nobel Prize for his work on animal behaviour.

The scent from a flower that has produced nectar travels through the air. It may stimulate the receptor cells of a honey bee and the insect flies towards it. As it gets closer, the bee also uses its eyes to find the flower. Its eyes are sensitive to ultraviolet light. This makes some of the pale markings we see in normal light stand out more distinctly to help the bee identify the flower. Some of the markings are lines running down the inside of the petal. They are called honey guides and direct the bee towards the nectar.

After landing on the flower the bee sticks its head between the stamens and probes the nectary with its mouth parts. While taking up the nectar it brushes past the anthers and pollen collects on the hairs of its back. When the bee has collected the nectar it flies on to the next flower and feeds again. Some of the pollen passes onto the stigma of the next flower.

The bee has stiff hairs on its front legs. Periodically it runs them through its body hair like a comb. This action collects the pollen off the bee's back and it is stored in structures made from hairs on its back legs called pollen baskets.

1 What attracts the bee to the flower? Which sense organs does it use?

2 How do you think that Karl von Frisch gathered information about the honey bee's behaviour?

3 How does the behaviour of the dancing bee help a colony of plants which have come into flower?

4 How do you think the hive of bees survive the winter when there are no flowers to feed on?

5 Why are hives of bees kept in orchards?

Figure A A bee in flight showing full pollen baskets.

When the bee swallows the nectar it collects in a cavity called the honey sac. The action of enzymes and the addition of other substances change the nectar into honey. After the bee has returned to its hive, it regurgitates the honey and passes it on to other bees working in the hive. They store it in the honeycomb. Also, the pollen is removed from the pollen baskets and stored.

The bee indicates the source of the nectar to the other bees in the hive by performing a dance on the honeycomb. The dance involves the bee moving in circles, waggling its abdomen and moving straight up and down on the vertical surface of the honeycomb. From this performance the other bees can tell the distance, direction and amount of nectar available and can set out to search for it.

For discussion

How useful are bees? Should we worry if there were fewer bees? Explain your conclusions.

Unusual methods of pollination

In Britain most plants are either insect or wind-pollinated. In different parts of the world there are variations in the way that flowers are pollinated. Here are just a few examples.

1 How could you arrange the unusual methods of pollination into groups?
2 Which flower acts as a trap?
3 Why do bat-pollinated flowers need to produce large amounts of nectar?
4 Which method carries the highest risk of failure?

Figure A The Bird of Paradise flower has stamens that form perches for birds. They pick up the pollen on their feet.

Figure B The century plant flowers contain large amounts of nectar for bats to drink. Each bat carries away the pollen on the fur on its head and neck.

Figure C A humming bird hovers in front of *Erythrina* sp. flowers while it probes into the flower with its beak to collect nectar. As it hovers it brushes its head on the stamens that are hanging outside the flower.

Figure D Honeysuckle flowers produce nectar at night to attract moths to pollinate them.

(continued)

Figure E   The cuckoo pint has male and female flowers on a short stem. There is a hood over the stem and the plant releases an unpleasant smell to attract small flies. The insects enter the hood and push through the downward-pointing hairs and over the female flowers. The stigmas of these flowers collect pollen from the insects. The hairs prevent the insects from leaving for a few days. During this time the male flowers make pollen. When they release it the hairs wither so that the insects can crawl over the male flowers, pick up the pollen and escape to take it to other cuckoo pint plants.

Figure F   Rafflesia is a parasitic flowering plant that lives on the roots of vines in the Malaysian rainforests. It produces a flower which is 91 centimetres across. This is the largest known flower of any plant. It is sometimes called the stinking corpse lily because of the smell of rotting meat that it produces to attract flies. There are separate male and female flowers and the flies they attract bring about pollination.

Figure G   Canadian pondweed produces male and female flowers on long stalks which let them reach the water surface. The male flower releases pollen onto the water and it floats away. Some of this pollen reaches the female flowers and pollination occurs.

Fertilisation

After a pollen grain has reached the surface of a stigma it breaks open and forms a pollen tube. The male gamete that has travelled in the pollen grain moves down this tube. The pollen tube grows down through the stigma and the style into the ovary. In the ovary are ovules, each containing a female gamete. When the tip of a pollen tube reaches an ovule the male gamete enters the ovule. It fuses with the female gamete in a process called fertilisation and a zygote (see page 123) is produced.

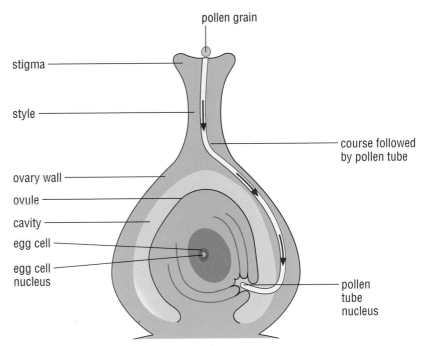

6 What is the difference between pollination and fertilisation?

7 Trace the path of a male gamete nucleus from the time it forms in a pollen grain in an anther until the time it enters an ovule.

Figure 8.10 Fertilisation.

After fertilisation

The zygote undergoes repeated cell division to form the embryo plant. Structures that later become the root and shoot are developed and a food store is laid down. While these changes are taking place inside the ovule the outer part of the ovule is forming a tough coat. When the changes are complete the ovule has become a seed. As the seeds are forming other changes are taking place. The petals and stamens fall away. The sepals usually fall away too but sometimes, as in the tomato plant, they may stay in place. The stigma and style wither and the ovary changes into a fruit.

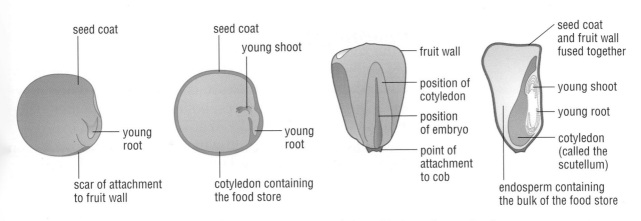

Figure 8.11 Parts of a pea seed.

Figure 8.12 Parts of a cereal grain.

Types of fruit

A fruit forms from the parts of the flower that continue to grow after fertilisation. There are two main types of fruit – dry fruits and succulent fruits.

Dry fruits have a wide variety of forms. They may form pods, such as those holding peas and beans, they may be woody nuts, such as acorns or hazelnuts, or grains like the fruits of wheat, oats and grasses.

Succulent fruits have a soft fleshy part. They may have a seed inside a woody skin which forms a 'stone' in the fruit, as in the cherry and peach. Many succulent fruits do not have a stone but contain a large number of smaller seeds, as in the tomato and orange.

Some fruits, such as apples, are called false fruits because their fleshy part does not grow from part of the flower but from the receptacle on which the flower grows.

Acorn cut open

Peach cut open

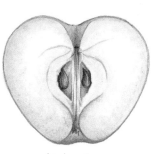

Apple cut open

Figure 8.13

Dispersing the fruits and seeds

A plant may produce many fruits. If they were all to fall to the ground around the plant the seeds inside them could eventually grow into new plants. There would be hundreds of new plants growing close together competing with each other for light, water and minerals in the soil, and so many would die. Overcrowding is prevented by fruit and seed dispersal. Plants use a range of ways to spread out their fruits and seeds so when new plants grow they are not competing with each other. The disadvantage of dispersal is that seeds may land in unsuitable surroundings, in which they fail to grow. However, plants produce large numbers of seeds to be dispersed to increase the chance of some of them reaching suitable surroundings where they may grow into new plants.

8 What are the differences between dry fruits and succulent fruits?

9 Summarise the text in a table to show how fruits and seeds are dispersed. Use the following terms: wind dispersal, animal dispersal, succulent fruits, hooked fruits, hard fruits, parachute fruits, winged fruits and explosive fruits. Give examples of each.

10 Why is a device that 'slows down the sinking speed' useful to wind-dispersed fruit?

11 Which kind of dispersal by animals provides the seeds with mineral salts (see also page 109)? Explain your answer.

For discussion

How could water be used to disperse fruits of some plants? Explain your answer.

How would the fruit have to be adapted to survive?

A few plants, such as the oak and the beech, have fruits that simply drop to the ground around them. Some of the acorns and beech nuts are collected and stored by squirrels and mice some distance from the tree. The animals eat most of these foods in their stores but some of the acorns and beech nuts may be left at the end of the winter. The seeds inside them may develop and eventually grow successfully into trees without competing with other seedlings or the parent tree.

Goose grass, burdock and agrimony have fruits with hooks on them. The hooks stick to the fur of passing mammals. They may be carried several kilometres before they are rubbed off and fall to the ground.

The flesh of succulent fruits often has a bright colour and is eaten by many different mammals and birds. If the seeds are small they are eaten with the flesh of the fruit. The seed coats are resistant to the digestive processes of the animal and the seeds leave the animal's body in the faeces. The large seed in the stone of a succulent fruit may also be dispersed by animals. It is not eaten but is thrown away when the animal finishes its meal.

Many seeds which have a small mass, such as the willow herb, develop long hairs. The hairs increase the air resistance of the seed and allow it to be blown away. The dandelion has a fruit that forms a tuft of hairs, which acts as a parachute and slows down the fruit's sinking speed as the wind blows it along.

Seeds with a larger mass that use air to disperse them have parts of their fruit shaped into a wing. The ash and the sycamore have winged fruits. The large surface area of the wing catches the wind as the fruit falls from the branches and allows it to be carried away from the tree on the air currents.

Some plants, such as the lupin and the gorse, produce pods which dry and twist. The tension in the twisting pod becomes so great that the pod splits open and shoots the seeds out.

hooks develop on the fruit coat

Goose grass

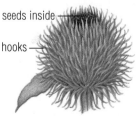

seeds inside

hooks

Burdock

Figure 8.14 Animal-dispersed fruits.

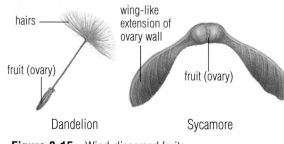

hairs

fruit (ovary)

Dandelion

wing-like extension of ovary wall

fruit (ovary)

Sycamore

Figure 8.15 Wind-dispersed fruits.

Life cycles

After the seeds have been dispersed they remain dormant in the ground until the conditions are favourable. At that point the embryo plant begins to germinate (see page 127). The life cycle of a flowering plant begins with a seed, which germinates and grows into a seedling. The seedling grows into a mature plant which produces flowers and later develops seeds. Many plants die after they have produced the seeds but some produce flowers and seeds for many years. This sequence of events is shown in Figure 8.16. The period of time between each of the main stages is represented by the letters A–D. The diagram can be used to show four different kinds of life cycle (see opposite).

Figure 8.16 Life cycle of a flowering plant.

1 Ephemerals, such as shepherd's purse, have a very short life cycle. All the stages A–D take place in only a few weeks then the plant dies. There may be more than one complete life cycle of an ephemeral plant in a year.

2 In annuals, such as the pea, all the stages A–D take place in the course of a year and the plant dies.

3 In biennials, A–D takes place over 2 years. In the first year the plant grows a set of leaves which make food that is stored over winter. The stored food is used together with the food made by the leaves in the following year to form the flowers and to make fruits and seeds. The carrot is an example of a biennial. It is harvested at the end of its first year for the food it has stored in its tap root.

4 In perennials, once the plant has flowered D occurs every year with further growth of the plant.

At the start of the life cycle

Most plants produce seeds towards the end of the year. The seeds usually lie in the soil throughout the winter. The inside of the seed is protected by a seed coat called the testa. It prevents insects biting through into the softer tissues beneath it. The testa also prevents fungi from entering and feeding on the store of food.

As more favourable conditions return in the spring the seed takes in water and the life processes, which have been taking place very slowly during the winter, start to speed up. As the soil warms up, enzymes that break down the starch in the food store begin to work. The starch forms the sugar that is used in respiration to release energy for growth of the tissues inside the seed. As the growth continues the seed coat breaks open and the root pushes its way out. With further growth the young shoot may push its way out or lift the rest of the seed to the surface (Figure 8.17). This process is known as germination.

The bean and the sunflower show two ways in which the shoot may grow. It may grow out from between the food stores as in the bean, or it may carry the food stores above the ground to form the first two leaves as in the sunflower.

12 It has been found from experiments that oxygen is needed for germination. Using the text, state two other external factors that are needed for seeds to develop.

13 How could you set up an experiment to investigate one of the factors you mention in answer to question 12?

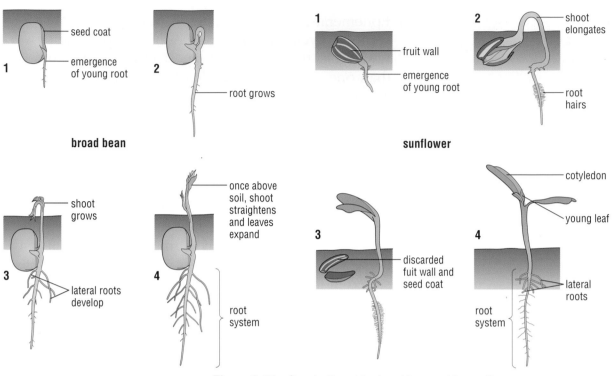

Figure 8.17 Germination of the broad bean and the sunflower.

14 Ink marks were placed at regular intervals along the root of a broad bean seedling but later the marks appeared as shown in Figure 8.18. What has happened?

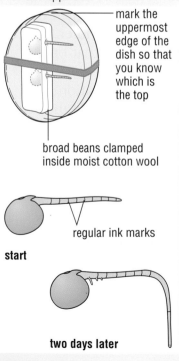

Figure 8.18

Perennials

There are two kinds of perennial plants – herbaceous perennials and woody perennials.

Herbaceous perennials

In herbaceous perennials the leaves wither at the end of the growing season. In the grasses some leaves are left above the ground, but in other perennials, such as the daffodil, all the leaves wither leaving no trace of the plant above the ground. The part of the plant that remains below the ground is called the perennating organ. Two common types of perennating organ are the bulb and the tuber.

Bulb

A bulb is formed on a disc-like stem. It is made from the swollen bases of the leaves. It contains food that was made by the leaves before they died. The food is used to provide fast, early growth in the spring so that the plant can produce its leaves and flowers before it has to compete with plants growing from seeds or with trees already in full leaf. The disc-like stem also contains buds which can develop into bulbs that split off and form separate plants.

15 How has the daffodil bulb developed from the plant shown in Figure 8.19?

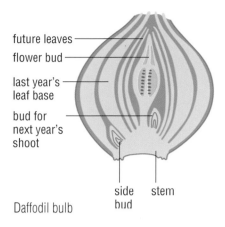

Daffodil plant

Daffodil bulb

Figure 8.19

Tuber

The buds on the lower part of a potato plant stem send out shoots that grow into the soil. The plant stores food in swellings along the underground shoot. These swellings are called tubers. In the potato plant we call them potatoes. At the end of the year the plant dies back but the tubers remain in the soil if not harvested. In the following year new plants grow from the tubers.

16 What do you think are the 'eyes' of a potato?

17 Why do you think potatoes go green when kept in the light?

18 How do you think the mass of the potato would change when it grew a new shoot and root? Explain your answer.

19 What experiment could you try to check your answers to question 18?

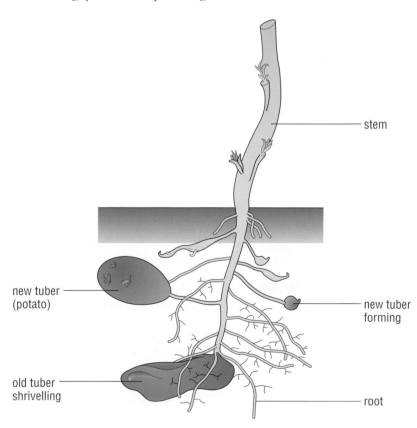

Figure 8.20 A potato plant.

Woody perennials

Trees and bushes are woody perennials. Although they may lose their leaves at the end of the growing season their stems remain above ground and increase in size every year.

Stem of a tree

There are two cylinders of dividing and growing cells in a tree's stem. The inner cylinder makes cells that form two types of tissue in the stem. On the inside the cells form xylem tissue and on the outside phloem tissue is made.

The cells in the xylem die and their cell walls break down to form long tubes called xylem vessels. Some xylem vessels carry water up the tree from the roots. Other xylem vessels nearer the centre of the tree form the heartwood which gives the tree support.

The outer cylinder of dividing cells encloses the phloem tissue. The phloem contains living cells that transport food up and down the tree. It also produces cells that make the bark. The bark forms a weather-resistant layer that protects the more delicate tissues beneath it from the harsh conditions of winter.

In the spring large xylem cells are produced. These in turn make wide xylem vessels. They are required to carry large amounts of water to the buds for leaf growth. During the summer, smaller xylem cells are made which in turn make narrower xylem vessels. At this time less water is required as the leaves are fully grown. In the autumn and winter the tree does not produce any xylem cells but the following spring large cells are made again. This making of different sized cells, year by year, leads to the ring pattern that can be seen in the trunk when a tree is felled. The number of rings can be used to estimate the age of a tree.

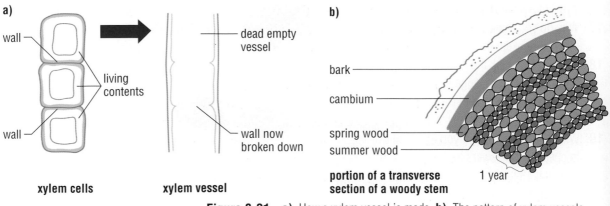

Figure 8.21   a) How a xylem vessel is made. **b)** The pattern of xylem vessels.

Figure 8.22   The annual rings made by a tree.

20 When bark is cut the phloem underneath is also damaged. How does this harm the tree?

21 How many years' growth can you see in the log in Figure 8.22?

22 How could you use the tree rings to estimate weather conditions in the past?

23 Why should there be a difference in the water demands of deciduous trees in spring and summer?

24 Trees exhibit a characteristic of life when they shed their leaves. What is it? Explain your answer.

Trees and leaf fall

Most broad-leaved trees produce their leaves in the spring. The leaves produce food throughout the summer and then are shed in the autumn. Trees that follow this pattern of leaf growth and loss are called deciduous trees.

Most coniferous trees and the broad-leaved holly lose and replace their leaves at all times of year and always appear in leaf. They are called evergreen trees.

Trees store waste products in their leaves before they release them.

◆ SUMMARY ◆

- ◆ The main features of a flower are the sepals, petals, stamens and carpels (*see page 114*).
- ◆ The stamen is the male part of the flower and is composed of the filament and anther (*see page 114*).
- ◆ The carpel is the female part of the flower and is composed of the stigma, style and ovary (*see page 114*).
- ◆ Pollination is the transfer of pollen from the anther to the stigma (*see page 117*).
- ◆ Wind and insect-pollination are the two main kinds of pollination (*see page 118*).
- ◆ Fertilisation is the fusion of the male gamete nucleus with the female gamete nucleus to form a zygote (*see page 122*).
- ◆ The ovule develops into a seed after fertilisation has taken place (*see page 123*).
- ◆ The ovary develops into the fruit after fertilisation has taken place (*see page 123*).
- ◆ Seed dispersal reduces competition between seedlings (*see page 124*).
- ◆ There is a range of ways in which seeds and fruits are dispersed (*see pages 124–125*).
- ◆ There are four kinds of plant life cycle (*see page 126*).
- ◆ Perennial plants live for many years. They may be herbaceous perennials or woody perennials (*see page 128*).

End of chapter questions

1 What is the difference between wind pollination and wind dispersal? Give an example of each.
2 How do animals disperse seeds?
3 What kind of life cycle would allow a plant to colonise an area of ground rapidly? Explain why you have made that choice and discounted the others.
4 How does the pH of water affect the growth of watercress? The pH of water in rivers varies. This experiment was set up to test the effect of pH on the growth of watercress.
   Seven petri dishes were set up. Each one had a solution of a different pH. The pH of the solutions is shown in the first column of Table 8.1.

Table 8.1

pH of growth medium	Initial number of leaves per shoot	Number of leaves after 14 days	Initial wet weight/g	Wet weight after 14 days/g
4.0	4	7	0.03	0.29
6.4	4	11	0.025	0.33
7.0	4	11	0.03	0.39
7.4	4	13	0.03	0.43
7.6	4	17	0.025	0.48
8.0	4	10	0.03	0.36
9.0	4	7	0.03	0.31

   a) In addition to weighing, how else were the plants examined after 14 days?
   b) Why were seven trials made instead of just one?
   c) Display in a graph how the number of leaves after 14 days varies with the pH of the water.
   d) Use the data on the initial weight and the weight after 14 days to calculate how much weight each plant gained in that time.
   e) Construct a graph of how the weight gain of the watercress varies with the pH of the water.
   f) Compare the two graphs you have drawn and write down what you see.
   g) How does the number of leaves on a plant affect its weight?
   h) What can you conclude from this experiment?

9 Looking at living things

The number of different kinds of living thing that have been identified on the Earth has reached 1.6 million. Some scientists think there may be a world total of up to 8 million different kinds of living thing, but we may never find them all.

In the rainforest

Over half of the different kinds of living thing on Earth are found in rainforests. The trees grow high and close together. Their crowns lock together and form a canopy. It is difficult for scientists to reach the canopy, but this is the place where most new kinds of living thing are discovered.

Rainforests grow close to the equator, in countries where the human population is growing rapidly. So, the forests are often destroyed to make way for homes, farms and roads. The wood that is cut down is being sold worldwide.

Every second a part of the rainforest is destroyed. Living things may be exterminated before scientists have even discovered them. In the past small groups of people lived in the rainforests. Today many of these groups have had to change their way of life as their rainforests have been destroyed. However, scientists have discovered that the people who still live in the forests know a great deal about the forest plants and may use them for medicines. This information is being used to discover ways in which rainforest plants can be used to provide medicines for the world population.

1 How many living things have been discovered in the rainforest:
   a) less than a million
   b) more than a million
   c) more than 2 million?
2 What makes the rainforest canopy?
3 Why is it difficult to discover new living things in the rainforest?
4 Why are rainforests being destroyed?
5 Why may some kinds of living things never be discovered?

For discussion

What steps must be taken so that all the rainforest wildlife can be identified?

What are the advantages and disadvantages of cutting down trees in the rainforests?

emergent

canopy

understorey

undergrowth

Figure 9.1   The layers of rainforest vegetation.

Figure 9.2 Ecologists using ropes to reach the canopy.

Signs of life

6 Which characteristics of life are shown by the mice in the pictures A–D in Figure 9.3?

If something is called a living thing it must have seven special features. These are called the characteristics of life. The characteristics are feeding, respiring, moving, growing, excreting (getting rid of waste), breeding, and irritability (being sensitive to the surroundings).

Animal life

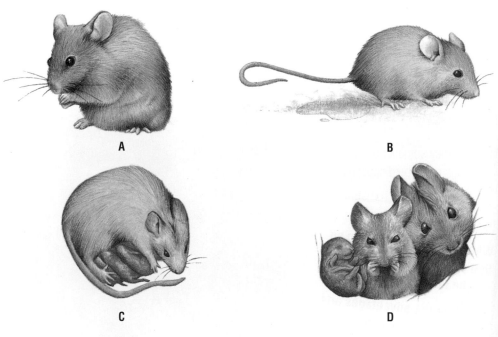

A

B

C

D

Figure 9.3 Four of the characteristics of life.

Plant life

Green plants make food from oxygen in the air and water by using energy from sunlight. Chemicals in the soil are also needed, but in very small amounts. All plant cells respire and gaseous exchange takes place through their leaves. Plants move as they grow and can spread out over the ground (see page 192). Wastes may also be stored in the leaves. Green plants are sensitive to light and grow towards it. Plants reproduce by making seeds or spores. Some plants reproduce by making copies of themselves.

Figure 9.4   Seedlings growing towards the light.

7   How is a green plant's way of feeding different from an animal's way of feeding?

(see page 192)

For discussion

A car can have five characteristics of life. What are they and how does the car show them?

If there are drought conditions, why might a plant produce seeds rather than grow new plantlets?

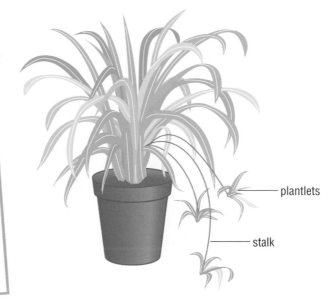

plantlets

stalk

Figure 9.5   A spider plant makes plantlets on stalks.

Life on Mars?

In 1976 two Viking spacecraft reached Mars. When they arrived each spacecraft split in two. One part, called the Orbiter, travelled around the planet taking photographs and measuring temperatures. The second part, called the Lander, touched down on the planet's surface. Although the Lander measured the Martian weather and had equipment on board to detect vibrations like earthquakes, the experiments that everyone wanted to know about were the ones to test the soil for signs of life. There was great excitement when one of the soil samples began to froth. It could have been caused by something respiring – a sign of life. After a few weeks of further investigation it was decided that the froth was most probably made by a chemical reaction not connected to a living organism.

There are signs that water once ran over the planet's surface, so some scientists believe that there could still be life there, but that it is buried deeper in the soil than the Lander could reach.

In 1997 the Pathfinder probe reached Mars and a vehicle called the Sojourner travelled around the landing site to take photographs and perform tests on rocks. It did not have any experiments on board to test for life. However, in future a probe may be able to bring back material from the surface of Mars so that scientists can investigate for signs of life.

1 What were the two parts of the Viking spacecraft and what did each part do?
2 Why could the froth be a sign that something was respiring?
3 What are the advantages and disadvantages of bringing back Martian rock to Earth to look for organisms?
4 Can any of the disadvantages be overcome? Explain your answer.

Classifying living things

Living things are put into groups so that they can be studied more easily. The largest groups are called kingdoms. Scientists have now named five kingdoms (see page 140). Each kingdom contains a large number of living things that all have a few major features in common. Table 9.1 shows the features that are used to place living things either in the animal or plant kingdoms.

Table 9.1 The features of living things in the plant and animal kingdoms.

Plant kingdom	Animal kingdom
Make their own food from air, water, sunlight and chemicals in the soil	Cannot make their own food. Eat plants and animals
Body contains cellulose for support	Body does not contain cellulose
Has the green pigment chlorophyll	Does not have chlorophyll
Stay in one place	Move about

The way that the animal kingdom is divided up into subgroups is described below. A similar way of subgrouping is used to divide up the living things in the other kingdoms.

Subgroups of the animal kingdom

Each kingdom is divided into groups called phyla (*singular*: phylum). Each phylum contains living things with more similarities. For example, in the phylum Arthropoda, which means 'jointed leg', all the animals have a skeleton on the outside of their body and have jointed legs. The phyla of the animal kingdom can be put into two groups called the invertebrates and the vertebrates. Invertebrates do not have an inside skeleton of cartilage or bone. Vertebrates do have an inside skeleton of cartilage or bone. The main phyla in the invertebrate group are the jellyfish, flatworms, annelid worms, arthropods, molluscs and echinoderms. There is only one phylum in the vertebrate group. It is known as the Chordata. The invertebrate and vertebrate groups are not actually part of the classification system but they are widely known and used to separate the animals in the Chordata from the animals in the other phyla.

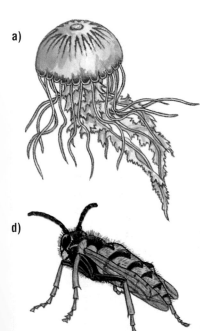
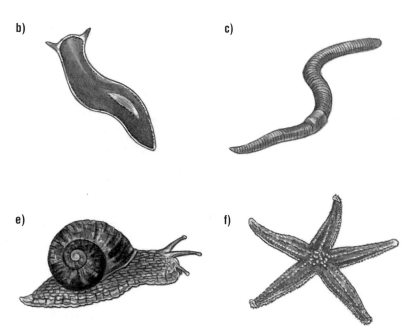

Figure 9.6 Examples of invertebrates. **a)** Jellyfish (compass jellyfish), **b)** flatworm (pond flatworm), **c)** annelid worm (earthworm), **d)** arthropod (wasp), **e)** mollusc (snail) and **f)** echinoderm (starfish).

Each phylum is divided up into groups called classes. The phylum Chordata contains seven classes that form the vertebrate group. The classes are jawless fish, cartilaginous fish, bony fish, amphibians, reptiles, birds, and mammals.

8 How is an earthworm different from a wasp, and how is it similar to a wasp?

Table 9.2 The features of five of the vertebrate classes.

Bony fish	Amphibians	Reptiles	Birds	Mammals
Scales, fins Eggs laid in water	Smooth skin Eggs laid in water	Scales Soft-shelled eggs laid on land	Feathers Hard-shelled eggs	Hair Suckle young with milk

9 How is a goldfish different from a frog, and how is it similar?

10 The insectivore in Table 9.3 is a shrew and the rodent is a mouse. How are they different and how are they similar to each other?

Each class is divided up into smaller groups called orders. The members of each order have so many features in common that they look alike and are easy to group. There are 19 orders of mammals. Four examples are shown in Table 9.3.

Table 9.3 Four orders of mammals.

Insectivores	Bats	Rodents	Whales
Small body Long snout	Small body Wings	Chisel-like teeth for gnawing	Flippers Tail with fins

An order is made up of smaller groups called families. The members of the different families look similar but there are differences. This can be seen by looking quite closely, as shown in the four families of whales.

Table 9.4 Four families of whales.

Beaked whale	Sperm whale	Dolphin	White whale
Few teeth, small flippers	Large head, rounded back fin	Sickle-shaped flippers and back fin	No back fin, blunt snout

11 How is a beaked whale different from a sperm whale?

12 How is a beaked whale similar to a sperm whale?

The members of a family have differences between them and are split up into smaller groups called genera (*singular*: genus). The differences between members of each genus are found by looking very closely. For example, if you look at dolphins A, B and C you will see that A seems to have more features in common with B than C. Because of this, dolphins A and B are placed in one genus and C is placed in a separate genus.

A Dusky dolphin

B White-sided dolphin

C Bottle-nosed dolphin

Figure 9.7   Members of the dolphin family.

Because dolphins A and B have small differences between them, they are placed in separate groups called species. A species is a group of animals that have a very large number of similarities and the males and females breed together to produce offspring that can also breed. The males and females of different species do not normally breed together, but when they do they produce offspring that are usually sterile (cannot breed). For example, a male donkey and a female horse produce a sterile mule.

13   How are dolphins A and B different from C?

14   How are dolphins A and B different from each other?

Setting up a system

In the 17th and 18th Centuries explorers were travelling the world in sailing ships and bringing back thousands of specimens of living things that had not been seen before by scientists. There was a great need for a system of grouping that everyone could understand.

Carl Linnaeus (1707–1778) travelled in Scandinavia, western Europe and England collecting and studying plants. He worked out a way of describing how one kind of living thing was different from another. He then began putting very similar living things into the same group. He gave each living thing two names. The first name was the name of its genus and the second name was its own specific name or species name. The names were made from Latin and Greek. These were two languages that scientists of every country learnt, so everyone could understand them. The words usually described the appearance of a living thing. For example, the genus and species name of the African clawed toad is *Xenopus laevis*. Xenopus is made from two Greek words – xenos meaning 'strange' and pous meaning 'foot'. The words refer to the toad's webbed hind foot which has three toes, each capped with a dark, sharp claw. The word 'laevis' is Latin for smooth and refers to the toad's smooth skin.

1 Why was there a need for grouping living things in the 17th and 18th Centuries?

2 What age was Carl Linnaeus when he died?

3 Why were Latin and Greek used to name living things?

For discussion
Why were the common names or local names not used in the scientific naming of plants and animals?

Other kingdoms of living things

As well as the animals, there are four other kingdoms of living things. They are the plants, Monera, Protoctista and fungi.

Plants

Plants are made from a large number of cells. Each cell has a cell wall made of cellulose. Plants make their own food by photosynthesis. The plant kingdom is divided into four groups.

Liverworts and mosses

Liverworts are small plants that do not have true roots, stems or leaves. They grow in damp places near streams and ponds.

Mosses have stems and leaves but they do not have proper roots. Moss plants are usually found growing together in many different habitats, from dry walls to damp soil.

Both liverworts and mosses reproduce by producing spores. They make the spores in a capsule that is raised into the air. When the capsule opens the spores are carried away by air currents.

Liverwort (*Pellia*)   Moss (*Polytrichum*)

Figure 9.8 A liverwort and a moss plant.

Ferns and horsetails

These plants have true roots and stems and reproduce by making spores. In ferns the spores are made in structures called sporangia on the underside of the large feather-like leaves called fronds. Horsetails produce a cone-like structure at the tip of the shoot that makes and releases spores. In both kinds of plant the spores are carried away by air currents.

Wood horsetail   Bracken fern

Figure 9.9 A horsetail and a fern.

Conifers

A conifer has roots, a woody stem and needle-like leaves. Most conifers lose and replace their leaves all year round, so they are called evergreen. Almost all conifers reproduce by making seeds that develop in cones. When the seeds are ready to be dispersed the cones open and the seeds fall out. Each seed has a wing that prevents the seed falling quickly and allows it to be blown away by the wind.

Figure 9.10 Male and female cones on a conifer.

Flowering plants

A flowering plant has a root, stem and leaves. In some plants the stem is woody. All of these plants reproduce by flowering and making seeds (see Chapter 8).

Figure 9.11 Grass, bluebells and these trees are all flowering plants.

Monera

Living things in this kingdom have bodies made from only one cell that has not got a nucleus. Living things in most other kingdoms are made from many cells that contain a nucleus at some stage of their development.

The two major subgroups of the Monera are the bacteria and the blue–green algae.

Bacteria

These are the smallest living organisms and are found in large numbers in every habitat. Some can photo-synthesise or process chemicals to obtain energy but most feed on the bodies and wastes of other living things. They either feed on the dead bodies of plants and animals or inside their living bodies where they may cause disease (see page 58).

Bacteria are classified according to their body shape. They may be round (cocci), rod-shaped (bacilli) or coiled (spirilla).

Blue–green algae

These cells either live on their own or form threads called filaments. They may also cluster together in a jelly-like substance that they make around themselves. Blue–green algae have other coloured pigments, including red and yellow. They live in seas, oceans and lakes, where they form part of the plankton (see page 107) and they make food by photosynthesis. They also grow on wet rocks at the sides of streams and rivers, at the top of rocky sea-shores and may occur widely in the soil.

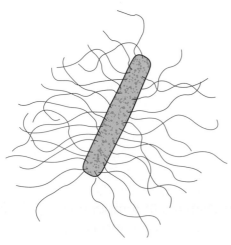

bacteria

blue–green algae

Figure 9.12

Protoctista

Many Protoctista have a body of just a single cell, although some are much bigger. They may move by making the substance inside their body flow. An *Amoeba* uses this method to form projections called pseudopodia which it uses to catch food. Other members of this kingdom may have a hair-like projection called a flagellum which they lash like a whip to move through water. Many Protoctista have bodies with small hair-like structures called cilia on their surface. They wave their cilia to-and-fro to push themselves through water.

Protoctista may either take in particles of food or make their own food by photosynthesis. Some live in the bodies of other living things and cause diseases, such as malaria and sleeping sickness.

Seaweeds are also part of the Protoctista kingdom. They have a body made from many cells.

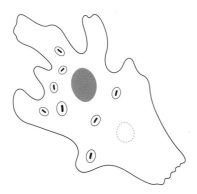

Amoeba

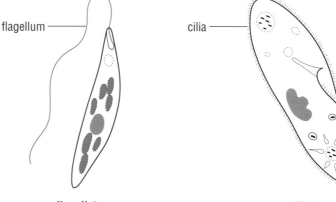

flagellate

ciliate

Figure 9.13

Fungi

Unlike plants, the cell wall of a fungus contains a substance called chitin. Many kinds of fungi can form very thin threads called hyphae. The hyphae feed on the dead bodies of plants and animals. As the hyphae grow they form a network called a mycelium. When the mycelium reaches a certain size it forms structures, called sporangia, that release spores. A spore is a reproductive cell with a thick wall around it. The wall provides protection from changes in temperature, prevents the cell from losing water in dry conditions and gaining water in wet conditions. In the white mould that grows on bread, the sporangia are black spheres. Each one grows on a thread from the mycelium.

In some fungi the threads join together to make a larger structure called a fruiting body. This may be divided into a stalk and cap as seen in mushrooms and toadstools. There are spore-producing structures called gills in the cap. The mycelium, which produces fruiting bodies, feeds in the soil or in rotting wood and is not usually visible.

A few fungi are parasites (feed on living things). Athlete's foot (see page 69) is caused by a fungus that feeds on the skin between toes.

Yeasts are fungi that do not produce hyphae. 'Wild' yeasts feed on the sugar that forms on the surfaces of fruits and in the nectar of flowers. From these 'wild' yeasts, special types have been developed for use in baking and making alcoholic drinks (page 43).

Figure 9.14 Fairy-ring mushroom. The fruiting bodies have been made at the edges of a disc-shaped mycelium in the soil.

15 In what ways are members of the Monera **a)** similar to and **b)** different from members of the Protoctista?
16 Why are fungi not placed in the plant group?
17 How could the plant kingdom be split into two subgroups according to the way they reproduce?

Viruses

Viruses do not have a cell structure. They can be stored like mineral specimens for many years without changing. During this time they do not feed, respire or excrete. When they are placed on living tissues they enter the living cells and reproduce. They destroy the cells in the process and may cause disease (see page 59).

For discussion
Are viruses living things? Explain your answer.

Speculating on life forms

Stars radiate heat and light energy. The Sun is a star and the Earth is at just the right distance for the amount of heat and light energy reaching it to drive living processes. Up until 1977 it was thought that all living things depended on energy from the Sun. In that year a new community of life forms was discovered. These organisms were living around 'smokers' at the bottom of the ocean. A 'smoker' is an underwater hot spring. It sends out black water that is rich in hydrogen sulphide. Bacteria around the vent use hydrogen sulphide as a source of energy, as plants use sunlight. Crabs and worms feed on these bacteria.

Figure A Worms around a black 'smoker' on the ocean floor.

1 What would happen to living things if the Earth moved
   a) nearer the Sun
   b) away from the Sun? Explain your answers.
2 How do you think a 'smoker' got its name?
3 What is unusual about the community of living things around the smoker?
4 Why did this discovery at the bottom of the ocean make scientists think there may be life in other places in the solar system?
5 How far should a planet be from its star if there is to be a chance of finding life forms similar to most of those found on Earth?

Today, space probes are being sent to investigate other planets and moons in the solar system. On two moons of Jupiter there are conditions that may be able to support living things. On one moon there is a great deal of hydrogen sulphide. Scientists are speculating on what life forms may have developed there.

Studies on stars show that some of them may have planets. Scientists have begun to think about the kinds of life that may be found on these planets.

For discussion
What kinds of life forms might you expect to find in other places in the solar system?

Keys

The way in which living things are divided up into groups can be used to identify them. The features about a phylum, class, order, family, genus or species can be set out as a spider key or organised as pairs of statements in a numbered key.

Spider key

On each 'leg' of the spider is a feature that is possessed by the living thing below it. A spider key is read by starting at the top in the centre and reading the features down the legs until the specimen is identified.

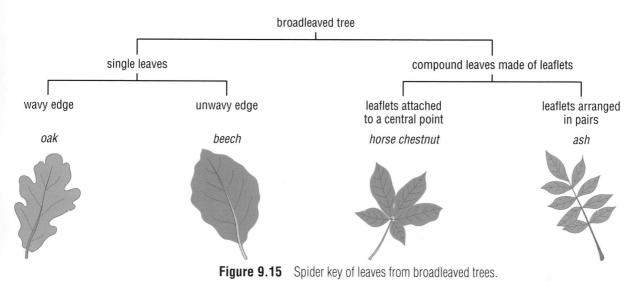

Figure 9.15   Spider key of leaves from broadleaved trees.

Numbered key

You work through a numbered key by reading each pair of statements and matching the description of one of them to the features you see on the specimen you are trying to identify. At the end of each statement there is an instruction to move to another pair of statements or to the name of a living thing. Here is a simple numbered key. It can be used to identify molluscs that live in freshwater habitats such as rivers, lakes and ponds.

18 Make a spider key for the four animals in Figure 9.16. Look carefully at the animals. Choose a feature they have all got in common to start at the top of the key.

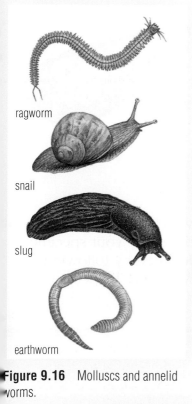

Figure 9.16   Molluscs and annelid worms.

1 a) Single shell .... see 2
  b) Two shells .... see 6

2 a) Snail with a plate that closes
       the shell mouth .... Bithynia
  b) Snail without a plate that
       closes the shell mouth .... see 3

3 a) Snail without a twisted shell .... Freshwater
       .... limpet
  b) Snail with a twisted shell .... see 4

4 a) Shell in a coil .... Ramshorn snail
  b) Shell without a coil .... see 5

5 a) Snail with triangular tentacles ..... Pond snail
  b) Snail with long, thin tentacles ..... Bladder snail

6 a) Animal has threads attaching
       it to a surface .... Zebra mussel
  b) Animal does not have threads
       attaching it to a surface .... see 7

7 a) Shell larger than 25 mm .... Freshwater
       .... mussel
  b) Shell smaller than 25 mm .... Pea mussel

19 Identify the molluscs A–F in Figure 9.17 using the numbered key on page 147. In each case write down the number of each statement you used to make the identification.

20 Why should another feature in addition to size be added to the statements in 7?

A

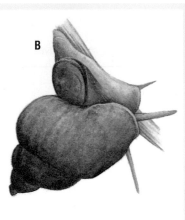

B

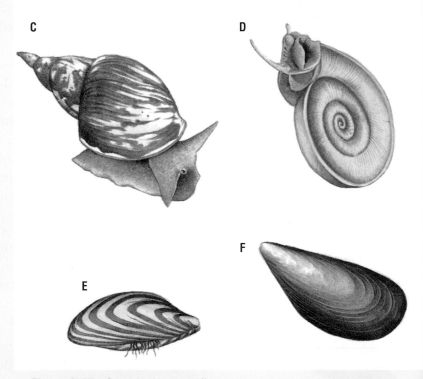

Figure 9.17 Some freshwater molluscs.

When using a numbered key write down the numbers of the statements you followed to identify your specimen. For example, specimen A is identified by following statements **1a**, **2b**, **3a**. It is a freshwater limpet.

21 Make up a numbered key to identify the arthropods in Figure 9.18. Begin by separating the butterfly, which has six legs, from the others.

millipede

centipede

crab

spider

butterfly

Figure 9.18 Arthropod specimens

22 Look at the parts of the insect's body in Figure 9.19a. Then look at how the parts vary among the six insect specimens in b. Invent a key to identify them.

23 Look at the numbered key for freshwater molluscs and the spider key for the leaves and answer the following questions.

   a) Which key identifies the larger number of living things?

   b) If both keys featured the same number of living things, which key would need the larger amount of space?

   c) What is an advantage of the numbered key?

   d) What is an advantage of a spider key?

   e) Which is the better one to use in a poster? Explain.

   f) Which is the better one to use in a pocket book for field work? Explain.

a)

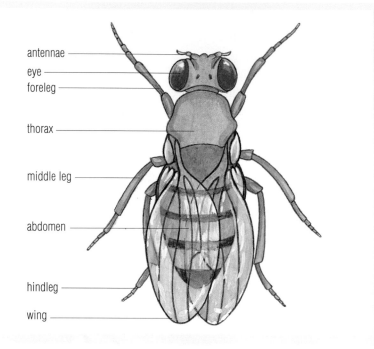

b)

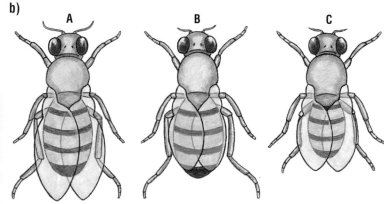

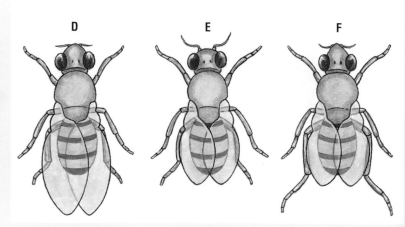

Figure 9.19

♦ SUMMARY ♦

♦ Over half the different kinds of living things on Earth are found in rainforests (*see page 133*).

♦ There are seven characteristics of life. They are feeding, respiring, moving, growing, excreting, breeding and irritability (*see page 134*).

♦ Living things are classified by putting them into groups. The groups are kingdom, phylum, class, order, family, genus and species (*see pages 136–139*).

♦ There are five kingdoms of living things. They are animals, Monera, Protoctista, fungi and plants (*see page 140*).

♦ Viruses do not have a cell structure (*see page 145*).

♦ Keys are used to identify living things (*see page 146*).

End of chapter questions

1 What kind of living organisms are the following:
  a) the cells are in jelly; makes food by photosynthesis
  b) have rod-shaped bodies and feed on dead plants and animals
  c) has a cell wall made of chitin and feeds on dead plants and animals
  d) has needle-shaped leaves
  e) produces a cone and releases spores from it
  f) has leaves and stem but does not have roots
  g) has a woody stem and flowers
  h) does not have a backbone but has five arms
  i) has a backbone and wings
  j) does not have a backbone but has wings
  k) has scales and lays eggs in water
  l) has scales and lays eggs on land
  m) has a backbone and hair?

2 The inside and outside of a house can provide a home for other living things besides humans and their pets. Is this true? Explain your answer.

10 *Variation and inheritance*

Variation between species

Figure 10.1   A cat, a rabbit and a South American monkey.

Many living things have certain features in common. For example, a cat, a monkey and a rabbit have ears and a tail. However, these features vary from one kind of animal to the next. In the species shown in the photographs, the external part of the ears of the rabbit are longer than the ears of the cat. The external part of the monkey's ears are on the side of its head while the other two animals have them on the top. The cat and the monkey have got long tails but the monkey's tail is prehensile, which means it can wrap it around a branch for support while it hangs from a tree to collect fruit. (Only monkeys that come from South America have prehensile tails.) A rabbit's tail is much shorter than the cat's tail and the monkey's tail. These variations in features are used to separate living things into groups and form a classification system which is used worldwide (see Chapter 9).

Variation within a species

The individuals in a species are not identical. Each one differs from all the others in many small ways. For example, one person may have dark hair, blue eyes and ears with lobes while another person may have fair hair, brown eyes and ears without lobes. Another person may have different combinations of these features.

Figure 10.2   Ears with and without ear lobes.

There are two kinds of variation that occur in a species. They are continuous variation and discontinuous variation.

Continuous variation

A feature that shows continuous variation may vary in only a small amount from one individual to the next, but when the variations of a number of individuals are compared they form a wide range. Examples include the range of values seen in different heights or body masses.

Discontinuous variation

A feature that shows discontinuous variation shows a small number of distinct conditions, such as being male or female and having ear lobes or no ear lobes. There is not a range of stages between the two as there is between a short person and a tall person. However, there are very few examples of discontinuous variation in humans.

For discussion

Look at this photograph of a family. What features do the members of the family have in common? Which features are found in more than one generation?

Figure 10.3   Members of a family.

Reproduction and variation

Information about how the body forms its features passes from one generation to the next during reproduction. The information is carried in genes, which are found on the chromosomes. Chromosomes are thread-like structures that appear in the nucleus of a cell when it divides.

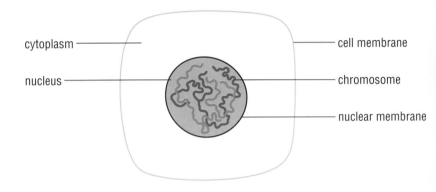

cytoplasm — — cell membrane

nucleus — — chromosome

— nuclear membrane

Figure 10.4   Chromosomes in a dividing cell.

There are two forms of reproduction. They are sexual reproduction and asexual reproduction.

Sexual reproduction

Usually two organisms, the male and female, are involved in sexual reproduction. Some flowering plants, however, have both male and female reproductive parts. As we have seen in Chapters 6 and 8 the male and female reproductive organs produce sex cells called gametes. In male animals the gametes are sperm cells. In the male part of the flowering plant the gametes are contained in the pollen grains. In female animals and the female part of a flowering plant the gametes are egg cells. In flowering plants each egg cell is contained in an ovule.

Sexual reproduction takes place when the nucleus of the male gamete fuses with the nucleus of the female gamete in the process of fertilisation. The zygote that is produced develops into the offspring. Genes from each parent are carried by the chromosomes in the nuclei of the gametes. The information that these genes contain controls the way the offspring develops.

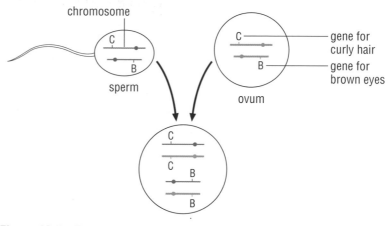

Figure 10.5 The positions of genes and chromosomes in animal gametes.

Dividing and mixing

Individuals of each species have a certain number of chromosomes in each of their body cells. In humans there are 46 chromosomes in each nucleus and they combine to form 23 pairs. When gametes are made in the reproductive organs the number of chromosomes is halved to 23 as they contain only one of each pair. If fertilisation takes place the zygote receives 23 chromosomes from the female gamete and 23 from the male gamete, so it will then have the correct number of chromosomes for development.

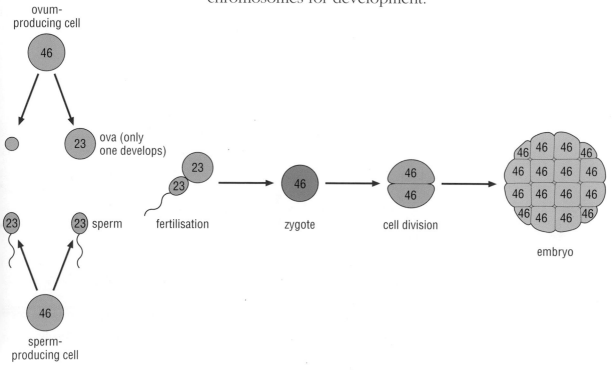

Figure 10.6 How chromosomes pair up at fertilisation.

When the chromosomes are dividing some of the genes on the chromosome may be altered. This produces an offspring that may have some features not found in either parent. This adds to the variation between the parents and the offspring.

How males and females are produced

One pair of chromosomes are the sex chromosomes. There are two sex chromosomes and in humans they have different lengths. The longer one is called the X chromosome and the shorter one is called the Y chromosome. Females have two X chromosomes and males have an X and a Y chromosome. When the male makes sperm cells each one receives either an X or a Y chromosome as the pair divides. All the eggs receive an X chromosome because female cells do not contain a Y chromosome.

When an egg meets a sperm at fertilisation it has an equal chance of meeting a sperm containing an X or a Y chromosome because the sperms with the different sex chromosomes are produced in equal amounts.

Asexual reproduction

Only one living thing is needed for this type of reproduction to take place. In the *Amoeba*, which is a member of the Protoctista kingdom, asexual reproduction takes place by the organism dividing into two. Firstly, the nucleus divides, then the cytoplasm divides. The two new individuals contain exactly the same genes as the parent organism and are exact copies of it.

1 What will be the sex of a baby produced when a sperm containing a Y chromosome fertilises an egg? Explain your answer.
2 Why do people not have two Y chromosomes?
3 Are girls or boys more likely to be formed after fertilisation? Explain your answer.

   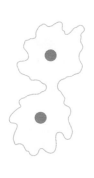 

parent *Amoeba* nucleus divides cytoplasm divides daughter cells separat

Figure 10.7 Stages in the division of an *Amoeba*.

Cells in a multicellular organism divide in a similar way to the *Amoeba* as the organism grows. For example, near the tip of a plant root there are cells that divide to produce new root cells.

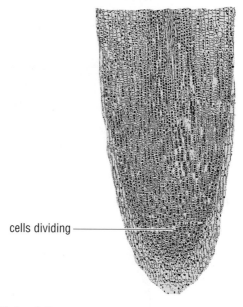

cells dividing

Figure 10.8 Cells at a growing point of a root.

Only a few animals reproduce asexually. *Hydra* is an example. It lives in ponds and ditches. It has a cylindrical body with an opening at one end surrounded by tentacles. The opening serves as a mouth but undigested food also passes out through it. *Hydra* feeds on small water animals by stinging them with special cells on its tentacles to paralyse them and then pulling them into its mouth. When *Hydra* is fully grown it may develop a bud that grows into another individual and separates from its parent.

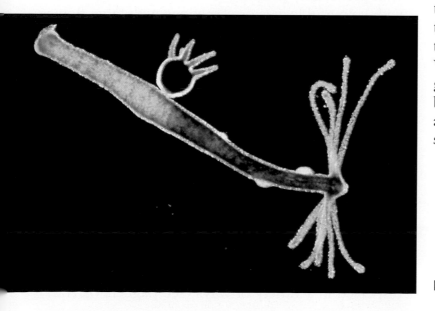

Figure 10.9 *Hydra.*

Many fungi reproduce by forming spores (see page 144). The spores are formed by asexual reproduction and each spore is capable of growing into a fungus like its parent. Yeasts are a type of fungus that do not produce hyphae and so do not form spores. They reproduce asexually by producing buds. Each bud may produce buds of its own before it has separated from its parent.

Figure 10.10 Yeast budding.

Some plants reproduce asexually naturally under certain conditions and sexually at other times. Gardeners can force some plants to reproduce asexually by artificial means. This is done to produce identical copies of plants with particularly pleasing features, such as geraniums with colourful leaves or carnations with large flowers.

Natural asexual reproduction in plants

Perennial plants like the daffodil have food storage organs that keep them alive through the winter and allow early growth in the spring. There are buds in the storage organ that are capable of growing into separate plants. The daffodil's storage organ is the bulb (see page 128) and the buds within it form small bulbs that separate from the parent plant. The new plants produced in this way are identical to the parent. There is no variation in the features between the parent and each of the new plants it has produced. However, the offspring produced by this method of reproduction have a greater chance of survival than plants that are produced sexually and dispersed in a variety of ways (see page 124). The dispersed offspring are much more likely to land in conditions in which they cannot grow, while the offspring produced asexually are further colonising an area in which the parent plant has grown successfully. The disadvantage of the plants growing close together is that they compete for water, minerals and light and may not grow as well as single plants.

Artificial asexual reproduction in plants

Many plants can be reproduced asexually by taking a cutting from them. The cutting is a small side-shoot. It is removed by making a cut with a sharp blade. The end of the cutting is dipped in rooting powder. This contains a hormone that makes the cells divide at the cut end. The cutting is then planted carefully in compost and it begins to form roots at the cut end.

Reproducing plants asexually makes sure that the new plants have all the features of the parent plant. However, it does not produce plants which have features that may be even more pleasing, such as more colourful leaves and flowers. The chance of these changes can only occur with sexual reproduction.

4 How would a family photograph be different from the one on page 153 if humans reproduced asexually?

5 Draw how three generations of yeast cells may appear under the microscope. Use circles to represent the parent and the buds.

6 A plant has grown successfully in a habitat. How does asexual reproduction help its offspring?

7 How could you get a large number of identical plants from just one plant?

Figure 10.11 Taking a cutting.

Variation and the environment

The environment can affect the features of a living organism. For example, if some seedlings of a plant are grown in the dark and some in the light they will have different features. Those grown in the dark will be tall,

8 How else could the environment affect the development of an organism? Give another example for a plant and an animal.

spindly and have small yellow leaves, while those grown in the light will have shorter, firmer stems with larger leaves that are green. Lack of food in the environment makes animals become thin. It can also slow down the growth of young animals.

Mendelian genetics

Gregor Mendel (1822–1884) was an Austrian monk who studied mathematics and natural history. He set up experiments to investigate how features in one generation of pea plants were passed on to the next. Pea flowers self-pollinate. When Mendel wished to control the way the flowers pollinated he cut off the anthers of one flower, collected pollen from another flower and brushed it on to the stigma of the first. He completed his task by tying a muslin bag around the first flower to prevent any other pollen from reaching it.

Mendel performed thousands of experiments and used his mathematical knowledge to set out his results and to look for patterns in the way that the plant features were inherited. He suggested that each feature was controlled by an inherited factor. He also suggested that each factor had two sets of instructions and that parents pass on one set of instructions each to their offspring. Many years later it was discovered that Mendel's 'factors' were genes.

Mendel's work was published by a natural history society but its importance was not realised until 16 years after his death. At that time Hugo de Vries (1848–1935), a Dutch botanist, had been studying how plants pass on their characteristics from generation to generation. He was checking through published reports of experiments when he discovered Mendel's work. De Vries's work supported Mendel's but he also made another discovery. He had studied the evening primrose, a plant that had been newly introduced into Holland, and found that the plants occasionally produced a new variety that was quite different from the others. This new variety was caused by mutation. Although mutations had been seen in herds of livestock before, where the odd animal was sometimes called a 'sport', de Vries was the first to introduce the idea of mutations into scientific studies. This led to its use in explaining evolution (see page 164).

1 Why did Mendel cut out the anthers of some flowers?
2 Why did Mendel tie a muslin bag around the flower in the experiment?
3 What is the value of performing a large number of experiments?
4 How did Mendel's conclusions about factors compare with the discovery of how chromosomes behave when gametes are made?
5 Could money be saved on fencing if you farmed short-legged sheep? Explain your answer.
6 Mutation means change. Why is it a good word to describe a new variety of a species?

Figure A   Short-legged sheep mutation.

DNA

Genes are made from a substance called deoxyribonucleic acid which is usually shortened to DNA. The first work on investigating the chemicals in cell nuclei was carried out by Johann Friedrich Miescher in 1869. He used the white cells in pus and the substance he discovered was called nuclein. Over the next 84 years generations of scientists made investigations on this substance. Rosalind Franklin (1920–1958) studied the structure of molecules by firing X-rays at them (see also Dorothy Hodgkin, page 71). In 1951 she investigated DNA in this way and her results suggested to her that it could be made of two coiled strands, but she was not sure. In 1953 James Watson and Francis Crick, using some of Franklin's results to help them, worked out that DNA is made from long strands of chemicals that are coiled together to make a structure called a double helix. The chemicals are arranged in a sequence that acts as a code. The code provides the cell with instructions on how to make the other chemicals that it needs to stay alive and develop properly.

Barbara McClintock (1902–1992) was a geneticist who studied maize – the plant that provides sweetcorn. While she was still a student she worked out a way of relating the different chromosomes in the nucleus to the features of the plant. Later, in the 1940s, she discovered that the genes on a chromosome could change position. They became known as 'jumping genes'. This discovery did not fit in with the way genes were thought to act and her work was not accepted by other scientists.

In the 1970s, during investigations by scientists on the DNA molecule, it was found that parts of the DNA broke off and moved to other parts of the chromosome. McClintock's work was proved to be correct and in 1983 she received the Nobel Prize for Physiology and Medicine.

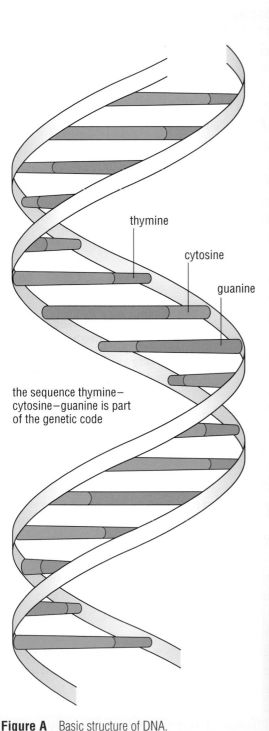

thymine

cytosine

guanine

the sequence thymine–cytosine–guanine is part of the genetic code

Figure A Basic structure of DNA.

Figure B Barbara McClintock.

(continued)

As each person's DNA is unique it can be used for identification purposes. A person's DNA profile (sometimes called a DNA fingerprint) can be made from cells in the saliva or the blood. The DNA is chopped up by enzymes and its pieces are separated into a gel in a process like chromatography. (Remember that chromatography is the process used to separate colours in an ink by putting a drop of ink onto a paper and allowing water to soak through it.) The pattern of the pieces looks like a bar code on an item of goods. Closely related people have more similar profiles than those who are not related.

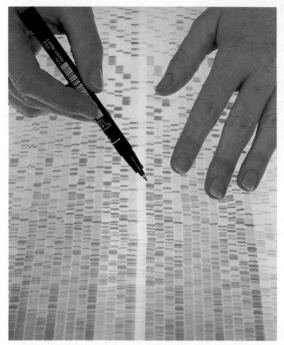

Figure C Examining a DNA profile.

For discussion

How could DNA be used to investigate a crime?

How firmly should scientists hold their views?

Selective breeding

For thousands of years people have been breeding animals and plants for special purposes. Most plants were originally bred to produce more food but later plants were also bred for decoration. Animals were originally bred for domestication, then for food production or to pull carts.

A breeding programme involves selecting organisms with the desired features and breeding them together. The variation in the offspring is examined and those with the desired feature are selected for further breeding. For example, the 'wild' form of wheat makes few grains at the top of its stalk. Individuals that produce the most grains are selected for breeding together. When their offspring are produced they are examined and the highest grain producers are selected and bred together. By following this programme wheat plants producing large numbers of grains have been developed.

Figure 10.12 'Wild' wheat (left) and modern wheat (right).

In some breeding programmes a number of features are selected and brought together. The large number of different breeds of dogs have been developed in this way.

9 All the different breeds of dog have been developed from the wolf by selective breeding. What features do you think have been selected to produce a greyhound? Give a reason for each feature you mention.

Figure 10.13 A wolf and a greyhound.

Evolution

After Carl Linneaus published his system of classification in 1735 (see also page 140) scientists could see that it could be used to suggest how living things were related and how some living things might have changed into others. Linneaus did not agree with them; he believed that everything developed at the same time.

Charles Bonnet (1720–1793) studied aphids. He found that females produced offspring from eggs that had not been fertilised. From his observations he believed that the offspring of every species was already preformed in the generation before and that the features in the species did not change. He also thought that fossils were the remains of living things that had been killed off by some catastrophe.

George Cuvier (1769–1832) worked on modifying the classification system of Linneaus. He also used it to classify fossils. He saw that there were many similarities and differences in the fossils found at different depths in the rocks. This made him think that the fossils were related to each other and to other living things, but he believed in Bonnet's catastrophe theory to explain why they had died.

Jean Baptiste Lamarck (1744–1829) also worked on improving Linneaus's system of classification and introduced the words 'invertebrate' and 'vertebrate' into classification. He tried to explain the relationships in the system of classification and in the fossils in the different layers of rocks. He put forward a theory of evolution in which he believed that one species gave rise to another over a long period. He suggested that evolution took place by an individual developing features that would help it survive and then passing these on to its offspring. He used the giraffe as an example. He thought that it had evolved from a species of antelope in which the individuals had developed stretched necks in order to reach leaves in higher branches. Scientists soon found many faults with Lamarck's theory but his work stimulated others to investigate the idea of evolution.

Charles Darwin (1809–1882) worked as a naturalist on the H.M.S. Beagle on its 5-year voyage around the world. The purpose of the voyage was scientific exploration. Darwin studied fossils of *Glyptodon* in South America and noticed that they were similar to giant versions of the armadillo that lived close by. He thought that the *Glyptodon* and the armadillo could be related.

On the Galapagos Islands, which are far from other lands, Darwin studied 13 different kinds of finches. He believed that they had all developed from one kind that reached the islands from distant lands a long time ago. He thought that they had evolved to feed on different foods (see Figure C).

When Darwin returned home with his specimens and his notebooks he worked on a theory to support his ideas. In 1858 he published this theory of evolution by natural selection with Alfred Russel Wallace (1823–1913). Wallace had also worked as a naturalist. He had visited the Amazon and Indonesia and had come to the same conclusions as Darwin. The theory they published is based on three facts and two deductions, as follows.

1. What would be the advantage of long-necked antelopes over short-necked antelopes?
2. An antelope could 'work at it' to stretch its neck. Could a frog 'work at it' to camouflage itself, and could a mole 'work at it' to get smaller eyes?
3. If Lamarck's theory was correct how would you expect the descendants of modern day body-builders to look in the future?

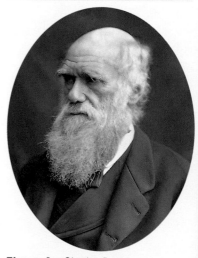

Figure A Charles Darwin.

Figure B Alfred Russel Wallace.

(continued)

Fact 1:   Plants and animals produce large numbers of offspring.
Fact 2:   The size of the population of plants and animals in one
                   place stays about the same.
Fact 3:   The individuals in each species vary.

Deduction 1:   The offspring must compete for the things they need, such
                   as food and water, and many must not survive.
Deduction 2:   The individuals that have variations most suited to survival
                   will do so and some will reproduce and pass on the
                   features that helped them survive.

The theory provides an explanation of how species change or evolve. The selection of features that lead to new species is similar to humans selecting features in farm crops or livestock. Here, however, the selection is through the natural way the species interacts with its environment. For this reason Darwin and Wallace described the process that brought about evolution as natural selection.

Darwin and Wallace did not know about genes, but when de Vries rediscovered the work of Mendel and added his own work on mutations, scientists could see a mechanism that would make evolution work.

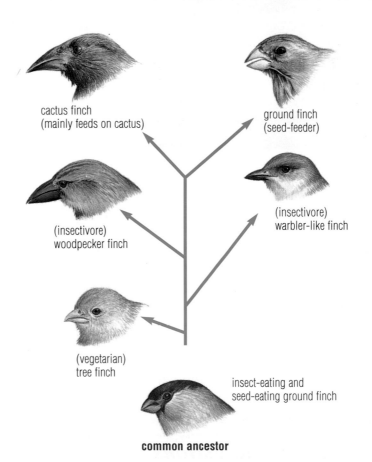

Figure C   Darwin's finches.

For discussion
How do you think the human species might evolve in the future? Explain your answer.

Clones

When you take a cutting you are making a clone. The cutting contains the same genes as the original plant. It will grow into an exact copy of the original plant.

In recent years ways have been found to clone animals. The nucleus is removed from an egg cell and is replaced by the nucleus of a normal body cell from the animal you wish to clone. The egg is then allowed to develop normally. An exact copy of the animal is produced. Dolly the sheep hit the headlines in 1997 as the first successfully reared clone.

Figure A   Dolly the cloned sheep.

For discussion

How could cloning help farming?

What disadvantages might there be to cloning farm animals?

If you were cloned today would your clone be just like you when it is your age? If not, why not?

◆ SUMMARY ◆

- ◆ There is variation between species (*see page 152*).
- ◆ There are two kinds of variation within a species. They are continuous and discontinuous variation (*see page 153*).
- ◆ Sexual reproduction leads to greater variation than asexual reproduction (*see pages 154–156*).
- ◆ Asexual reproduction occurs in many groups of living things. Offspring are genetically identical to the parent (*see page 156*).
- ◆ The environment can affect the variation in a species (*see page 159*).
- ◆ New varieties of a species can be produced by selective breeding (*see page 162*).

End of chapter questions

1 What kind of reproduction – sexual or asexual – can lead to the evolution of a species? Explain your answer.
2 Investigating camouflage. Garden birds were given different coloured food pellets against different coloured backgrounds to test the effect of camouflage. The food pellets were made of flour and lard and were coloured with harmless dyes. The pellets represented prey animals and were coloured either green or brown. The prey were tested against three backgrounds – grey, green and brown. The backgrounds were painted on 50 cm square aluminium sheets.

(continued)

Twenty-four trials were made, twelve with grey backgrounds and six each with green and brown backgrounds. In each trial two backgrounds of the same colour were set up a metre apart in a garden. Ten green and ten brown prey were placed on each sheet. When half the prey had been eaten by the garden birds the trial was stopped and the numbers of green and brown prey that had been eaten were recorded. The trials with pairs of coloured backgrounds were made in a random order. The results of the trials are displayed in Table 10.1.

Table 10.1

Grey background				Green background		Brown background	
Numbers eaten		Numbers eaten		Numbers eaten		Numbers eaten	
Green	Brown	Green	Brown	Green	Brown	Green	Brown
18	10	8	19	6	17	11	2
11	8	14	5	0	11	10	2
8	13	7	11	15	4	19	1
12	4	15	6	12	12	5	7
18	9	14	4	12	19	12	8
4	12	18	17	11	9	5	11
Grand totals:		147	118	56	72	62	31

a) Why were two backgrounds used in each trial?

b) Why were the backgrounds mixed up at random and not put out as grey twelve times, green six times and brown six times?

c) Was green or brown prey more likely to be eaten on the grey background?

d) Identify any pairs of numbers that do not follow this trend.

e) What percentage of green prey are eaten on a grey background?

f) What is the percentage of green prey eaten on **i)** a green background and **ii)** a brown background?

g) How might you have expected the results on the green background to be different from those in the table?

h) Do the colours of the prey help to camouflage them? Explain your answer.

11 Living things in the environment

If you look out across the countryside you may see fields, hedges, woods, ponds and maybe a river. Most of the living things you see will be plants ranging in size from green slime on rocks to the tallest tree in a wood. You may see some birds flying across the countryside and a few insects moving through the air around you. There may be a slug slowly moving across your path or a squirrel scampering away through the branches of a nearby tree. The scene may look too complicated to investigate scientifically but the study of ecology was established at the beginning of the 20th Century to do just this.

Ecology means the study of living things and where they live. The home area of a living thing is called its habitat. Two examples of habitats are a wood and a pond. The country scene in Figure 11.1 can be divided into a number of different habitats for further investigation.

1 What habitats can you see in Figure 11.1?

Figure 11.1 A countryside scene from a hilltop showing a range of habitats.

A living thing in its habitat is affected by two different kinds of factors. They are abiotic factors and biotic factors. Abiotic factors are not due to living things and include temperature, wind strength, amount of light and moisture. Biotic factors are due to living things and include plants and animals as sources of food, other organisms competing for space, and predators.

Recording the plant life in a habitat

When a habitat is chosen for study a map is made in which the habitat boundaries and major features, such as roads or cliffs, are recorded. The main kinds of plants growing in the habitat are identified and the way they are distributed in the habitat are recorded on the map.

A more detailed study of the way the plants are distributed is made by using a quadrat and by making a transect.

Using a quadrat

A quadrat is a square frame. It is placed over an area of ground and the plants inside the frame are recorded. If there are only a few plants in the quadrat, as may occur if it is placed on waste ground, the positions of the individual plants can be recorded in a diagram of the quadrat. If the quadrat is placed in an area with a large number of plants covering the ground, such as in a lawn, the area occupied by each type of plant is estimated. For example, a quadrat on a lawn may show the plants to be 90% grass, 7% daisy and 3% dandelion.

Figure 11.2 Ecologists mapping a habitat.

When using a quadrat the area of ground should not be chosen carefully. A carefully selected area might not give a fair record of the plant life in the habitat but may support an idea that the ecologists have worked out beforehand. To make the test fair the quadrat is thrown over the shoulder so that it will land at random. The plants inside it are then recorded. This method is repeated a number of times and the results of the random samples are used to build up a record of how the plants are distributed. An estimate of how many of each kind there is in the area can then be made.

2 How could you use a quadrat to see how the plants change in a particular area over a year?

Figure 11.3 Ecologists using a quadrat.

Making a transect

If there is a feature such as a bank, a footpath or a hedge in the habitat, the way it affects plant life is investigated by using a line transect. The position of the transect is chosen carefully so that it cuts across the feature being examined.

The transect is made by stretching a length of rope along the line to be examined and recording the plants growing at certain intervals (called stations) along the rope. When plants are being recorded along a transect, abiotic factors such as temperature or dampness of the soil may also be recorded to see if there is a pattern between the way the plants are distributed and the varying abiotic factors.

Figure 11.4 Ecologists making a transect.

3 How useful do you think quadrats and line transects are for recording the positions of animals?

4 Which method – quadrat or transect – would be more useful for investigating the plants growing around the water's edge of a pond? Explain your answer.

5 Look at the results from a line transect shown in Table 11.1.

Table 11.1

Station	1	2	3	4	5	6	7	8	9	10
Soil condition	W	D	W	W	D	Dr	Dr	Dr	D	Dr
Plant present	A	A	B	A	B	C	C	C	B	C

W = very wet soil; D = damp soil; Dr = dry soil

What can you say about the plants in this habitat from the information in these results?

Collecting small animals

Different species of small animals live in different parts of a habitat. In a land habitat they can be found in the soil, on the soil surface and leaf litter, among the leaf blades and flower stalks of herbaceous plants, and on the branches, twigs and leaves of woody plants. They can be collected from each of these regions using special techniques.

Collecting from soil and leaf litter

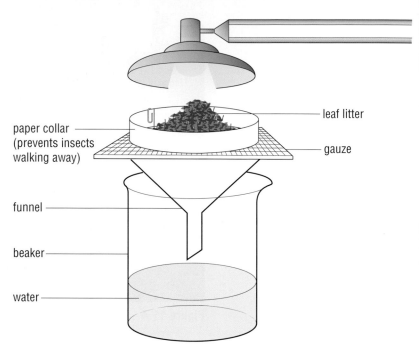

paper collar
(prevents insects
walking away)

leaf litter

gauze

funnel

beaker

water

Figure 11.5 A simple Tullgren funnel.

A Tullgren funnel is used to collect small animals from a
sample of soil or leaf litter. The sample is placed on a
gauze above the funnel and a beaker of water is placed
below the funnel. The lamp is lowered over the sample
and switched on. The heat from the lamp dries the soil
or leaf litter and the animals move downwards to the
moister regions below. Finally, the animals move out of
the sample and into the funnel. The sides of the funnel
are smooth so the animals cannot grip onto them and
they fall into the water.

Pitfall trap

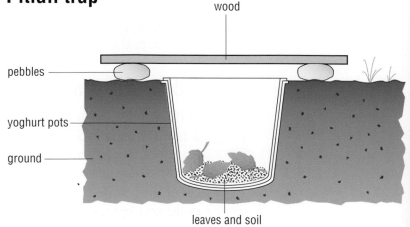

wood

pebbles

yoghurt pots

ground

leaves and soil

Figure 11.6 A pitfall trap.

The pitfall trap is used to collect small animals that move over the surface of the ground. A hole is dug in the soil to hold two containers, such as yoghurt pots, arranged one inside the other. The containers are placed in the hole and the gap around them up to the rim of the outer container is filled in with soil. A few small leaves are placed in the bottom of the container and four pebbles are placed in a square around the top of the trap. A piece of wood is put over the trap, resting on the pebbles. The wood makes a roof to keep the rain out and hides the container from predators. When a small animal falls in it cannot climb the smooth walls of the inner container and remains in the trap, hiding under the leaves until the trap is emptied. Traps must be emptied after a few hours and those set in the evening must be emptied the following morning. The animals are collected by removing the cover, taking up the inner container and emptying it into a white enamel dish. The animals can be seen clearly against the white background and identified.

6 What is the advantage of using an outer and an inner container instead of just one container for the pitfall trap?

7 Why are large leaves not used inside the trap?

Sweep net

Figure 11.7 Using a sweep net.

The sweep net is used to collect small animals from the leaves and flower stems of herbaceous plants, especially grasses. The lower edge of the net should be held slightly forward of the upper edge to scoop up the animals as the net is swept through the plants. After one or two sweeps the mouth of the net should be closed by hand and the contents emptied into a large plastic jar where the animals can be identified.

Sheet and beater

Small animals in a bush or tree can be collected by setting a sheet below the branches and then shaking or beating the branches with a stick. The vibrations dislodge the animals, which then fall onto the sheet. The smallest animals can be collected in a pooter (Figure 11.8).

Pooter

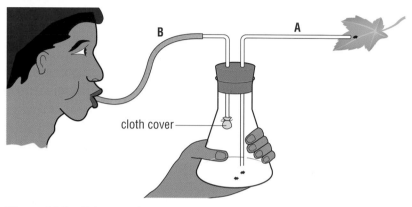

Figure 11.8 Using a pooter.

8 What is the purpose of the cloth on tube B of the pooter?

Tube A of the pooter is placed close to the animal and air is sucked out of tube B. This creates low air pressure in the pooter so that air rushes in through tube A carrying the small animal with it.

Collecting pond animals

Pond animals may be collected from the bottom of the pond, the water plants around the edges or the open water just below the surface.

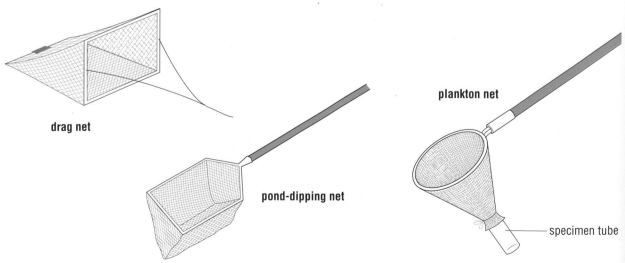

Figure 11.9 Three types of pond net.

A drag net is used to collect animals from the bottom of the pond. The net is dragged across the bottom of the pond. As it moves along it scoops up animals living on the surface of the mud. The pond dipping net is used to sweep through vegetation around the edge of the pond to collect animals living on the leaves and stems. A plankton net is pulled through the open water to collect small animals swimming there.

The drag and pond dipping nets are emptied into white enamel dishes so that the animals can be identified and studied. The dishes should be set up out of full sunlight so that the water does not get hot, and they should be emptied back into the pond as soon as the investigation is complete. The plankton net has a small bottle that is examined with a hand lens. Samples are then taken for microscope examination.

Adaptation

A living thing survives in its habitat because it can cope with the abiotic and biotic factors. It copes if its body is adapted to the conditions of the habitat. Changes that have taken place in the structures of different species over time that help them survive are called adaptations.

Some adaptations in plants

Grass

One of the commonest land plants is grass. Unlike many plants it survives in areas where there are grazing animals. Grass has growing points that are below the reach of the grazers' mouths. This means that when most of the leaves of the grass are removed and eaten, the growing points can produce new leaves. The grazing animals also eat the grass flowers but the grass can also reproduce asexually by sending out side-shoots, called tillers, that grow along or just below the soil surface. Buds along the tiller produce new grass plants. The colony produced in this way binds with the soil to form turf which is hard wearing and is not destroyed by the feet of the grazing animals. These adaptations allow the grass to survive.

9 Why do the low growing points of grasses help them to survive?

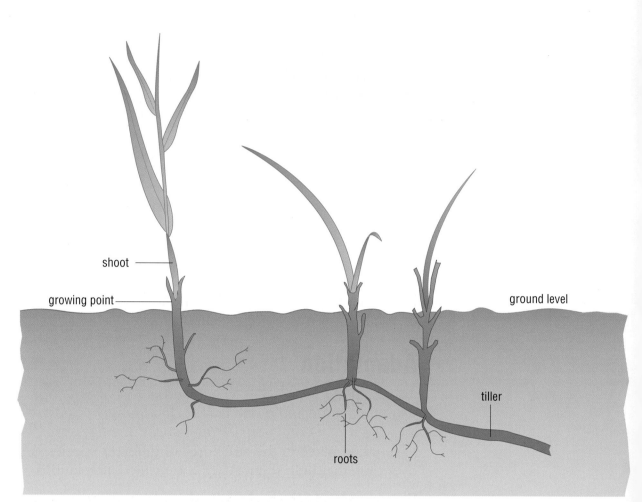

Figure 11.10 A grass plant.

Water plants

10 In what ways are the features of a plant living in water different from a plant living on land?

The roots of land plants have oxygen around them in the air spaces in the soil. In the waterlogged mud at the bottom of a pond there is very little oxygen for the root cells. The stems of water plants have cavities in them through which air can pass to the roots in order to overcome this problem.

Water plants use the gases they produce to hold their bodies up in the water and therefore do not need strong, supporting tissues like land plants. Minerals can be taken in from the water through the shoot surfaces of the water plant, leaving the root to act as an anchor. The leaves of submerged water plants are thin, allowing minerals in the water to pass into them easily. The leaves also have feathery structures that make a large surface area in contact with the water. This further helps the plant to take in all the essential minerals.

Floating water plants like duckweed have a root that acts as a stabiliser.

Figure 11.11   A pond with a range of water plants.

Seasonal adaptations in plants

The abiotic factors in a habitat change with the seasons. The grass plant is adapted to survive winter conditions but its short roots make it dependent upon the upper regions of the soil staying damp. In drought conditions the soil dries out and the grass dies. Daffodils (see page 129) are adapted to winter conditions as the leaves above the ground die and the plant forms a bulb in the soil. Bark is an adaptation of trees that provides a protective insulating layer around the woody shoot in winter.

Plants that float on the open water of a pond in spring and summer do not remain there in the winter. Duckweed produces individuals that sink to the pond floor; the water plant called frogbit produces heavy seeds. The plants around the water's edge die back and survive in the mud as thick stems called rhizomes.

Some adaptations in animals

Land animal

The tawny owl has adaptations that allow it to catch mice at night. It has large eyes that are sensitive to the low intensity of light in the countryside at night. These allow it to see to fly safely. The edges of some of the owl's wing feathers are shaped to move noiselessly through the air when the bird beats its wings. This prevents the mouse's keen sense of hearing detecting the owl approaching in flight. The owl has sharp talons on its toes that act as daggers, to kill its prey quickly and to help carry the prey away to be eaten at a safe perch.

11 In what ways are plants adapted to survive winter conditions?

12 What adaptations does the tawny owl have that allow it to detect its prey, approach its prey and attack its prey?

13 Why should the owl kill its prey quickly?

14 What adaptations do you think a mouse may have to help it survive a predator's attack?

Figure 11.12 A tawny owl, swooping down on a wood mouse.

Water animal

Although it lives underwater the diving beetle breathes air. It comes to the surface and pushes the tip of its abdomen out of the water. The beetle raises its wing covers and takes in air through breathing holes, called spiracles, on its back. (In insects living on land the spiracles are on the side of the body.) When the beetle lowers its wing covers more air is trapped in the hairs between them. It is able to breathe this air while it swims underwater. Diving beetles feed on a range of foods, including small fish, tadpoles and other insects.

Figure 11.13 A diving beetle feeding on an earthworm.

Seasonal adaptations in animals

The roe deer lives in woodlands. In the spring and summer when the weather is warm it has a coat of short hair to keep it cool. In the autumn and winter it grows longer hair that traps an insulating layer of air next to its skin. This reduces the loss of heat from its body.

The stoat grows a white coat in the winter which loses less heat than its darker summer coat. The stoat preys on rabbits and its white coat may also give it some camouflage when the countryside is covered in snow.

The ptarmigan is about the size of a hen. It lives in the north of Scotland, northern Europe and Canada. In summer it has a brown plumage that helps it hide away from predators while it nests and rears its young. In winter it has a white plumage that reduces the heat lost from its body and gives it camouflage. Feathers grow over its toes and make its feet into snowshoes which allow it to walk across the snow without sinking.

15 How do the adaptations of **a)** the roe deer, **b)** the stoat and **c)** the ptarmigan help them survive in the winter?

16 How might their winter adaptations affect their lives if they kept them through the spring and summer?

A roe deer in summer

A ptarmigan in winter

Figure 11.14

Studying animals more closely

After a habitat has been surveyed and the different species of plants and animals identified and recorded, further studies about their lives can be made. These involve making observations. If the species to be studied is a plant, a record of its growth, flowering and seed dispersal may be made. If the species is an animal, its

17 Why do you think bird-watching is a popular hobby?

18 Why should laboratory observations be compared with observations of animals in their habitat?

behaviour may be observed over different times of the day and throughout the year. Birds are relatively easy to study because most species do not hide away. Small animals hide away but they can be kept in containers in the laboratory for their activities to be observed. Any observations made in the laboratory must be compared to observations of animals living in their habitat before any firm conclusions are drawn and the laboratory animals should be returned to their habitat as soon as all the observations on them are complete.

Animals in the laboratory

Small animals can be studied in the laboratory or animal house by setting up a habitat that is similar to their own.

Snails

Snails can be kept in an aquarium tank. The floor of the tank should be covered with a mixture of damp soil and peat. Large stones may be placed in the mixture for the snails to climb on and hide under.

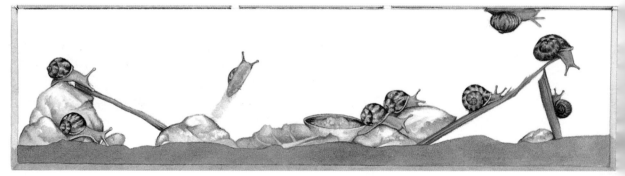

Figure 11.15   A snail tank.

Woodlice

Woodlice can also be kept in an aquarium tank if the floor is covered with soil and a layer of damp moss and pieces of bark.

Figure 11.16   A woodlouse tank.

19 The woodlice were also observed in damp conditions but not in dry ones. How would you set up the shallow tray to test this observation?

20 When checking the behaviour of the woodlice in their habitat some were found under a log one day and under a stone about a metre away the next day. When do you think they moved? Explain your answer.

Investigating behaviour

Experiments can be devised to investigate the way the animals behave after observing them in the tanks. For example, it may be noticed that the woodlice are found under the bark in the daytime. This observation may lead to the idea that woodlice do not like the light. This idea can be tested by putting the woodlice in a shallow tray, part of which is uncovered and in the light and part of which is covered and in the dark. The woodlice should be placed in the centre of the tray and left for a few minutes before recording where they have settled to rest.

Looking for links between animals and plants

All the individuals of a species in a particular habitat make up a group called a population. All the populations of the different species in the habitat make up a group called a community. Ecologists look for links between the animals and plants in the community to understand how they live together.

Most animals spend a large part of their time searching for food. By observing animals in their habitat the food of each species can be identified.

Living things can be grouped according to how they feed. Plants make their own food by photosynthesis and by taking in minerals. They are called the producers of food. Animals that feed on plants are called primary consumers. They are also known as herbivores. Animals that feed on primary consumers are called secondary consumers. They are also known as carnivores. The highest level consumer in a food chain (see page 182) is called the top carnivore. Animals that feed on plants and animals are called omnivores. They feed as a primary consumer when they feed on plants and as a secondary or higher level consumer when they feed on animals.

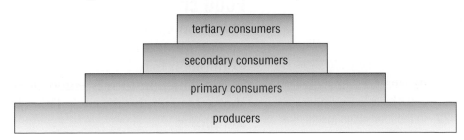

Figure 11.17 This diagram shows how the number of producers and consumers compare in a habitat. The bigger the block, the bigger the number of animals in a habitat.

Special relationships

A predator is a carnivore and the animal that it feeds on is its prey. A predator may have a wide range of prey. A weasel, for example, feeds on frogs, mice, voles, rats, small birds and moles. In the prey–predator relationship the predator survives by killing the prey. Young, old or sickly prey are the easiest animals to catch. The prey may sometimes try to avoid being caught by having camouflage or being able to move fast.

A parasite lives on or in another organism and feeds on it. The organism that contains the parasite is called the host. A head louse is an ectoparasite. It lives on the outside of the body and feeds on blood by piercing the skin on the scalp. The tapeworm is an endoparasite. It lives in the small intestine and feeds on the digested food. In the parasite–host relationship both organisms stay alive but the host is harmed (sometimes fatally) by the presence of the parasite. Some fungi are parasites on green plants and frequently kill them. Mistletoe is a green plant that is a semi-parasite. It has green leaves and can photosynthesise but it takes its minerals from the apple or poplar tree on which it is growing.

There are some organisms that are able to live apart but benefit when they live together. This relationship is called commensalism. Feeding may be only a part of this relationship. For example, the hermit crab often has sea anemones on its shell. They provide it with some camouflage and the messy feeding habits of the crab makes a cloud of food particles in the water that the sea anemones can feed on.

Mutualism is a relationship where both organisms need each other to survive. The termite feeds on wood, which is made of cellulose. Protoctista that make an enzyme to digest cellulose live in the termite's gut. They allow the termite to digest the wood and in return the termite provides them with a home. The lichen is another example of mutualism. It consists of a fungus and an algae growing together. The fungus provides the support in which the algae can grow. The algae makes food by photosynthesis using the water that the fungus has stored. The fungus also takes in minerals to be converted into materials for growth. Together the two organisms form a structure that can live on the surfaces of rocks in harsh conditions where other organisms cannot survive.

1 Write down six examples of predators and their prey. For each pair say how each animal is adapted to catch prey or avoid being eaten.
2 Why is it a disadvantage if the parasite kills the host?
3 Why is mistletoe called a semi-parasite?
4 What is the difference between commensalism and mutualism?
5 How might a predator help the population of its prey?

Figure A   Head louse.

Figure B   Hermit crab with sea anemones on its shell.

Food chains

21 In the food chain identify
   a) the primary consumer,
   b) the secondary consumer
   and **c)** the tertiary consumer.
22 In the food chain identify the herbivore and the carnivores.

The information about how food passes from one species to another in a habitat is set out as a food chain. For example, it may be discovered that a plant is eaten by a beetle which in turn is eaten by a shrew and that the shrew is eaten by an owl. This information can be shown as follows:

plant → beetle → shrew → owl

23 Construct some food chains with humans in them.

24 In the food chains you have constructed are humans classed as herbivores, carnivores or omnivores?

Once a food chain has been worked out further studies can be done on the species in it.

Ecological pyramids

The information about each species in the food chain can be displayed in a diagram called an ecological pyramid.

Pyramid of numbers

The simplest type of ecological pyramid is the pyramid of numbers. The number of each species in the food chain in a habitat is estimated. The number of plants may be estimated using a quadrat (see page 169). The number of small animals may be estimated by using traps, nets and beating branches (see pages 172–174). The number of larger animals, such as birds, may be found by observing and counting.

An ecological pyramid is divided into tiers. There is one tier for each species in the food chain. The bottom tier is used to display information about the plant species or producer. The second tier is used for the primary consumer and the tiers above are used for other consumers in the food chain (see Figure 11.17). The size of the tier represents the number of each species in the habitat. If the food chain:

$$grass \rightarrow rabbit \rightarrow fox$$

is represented as a pyramid of numbers, it will take the form shown in Figure 11.18.

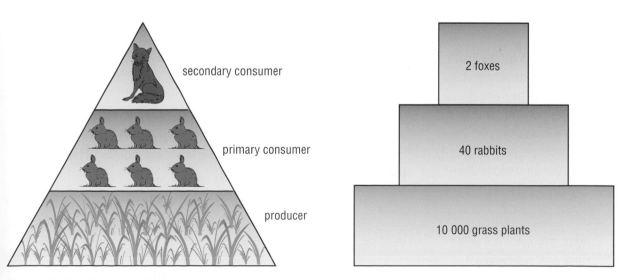

Figure 11.18 Food pyramid of numbers of grass plants, rabbits and foxes.

25 What would happen to the number of rabbits and grass plants if the number of foxes
a) increased and
b) decreased?

26 What would happen to the number of grass plants and foxes if the number of rabbits
a) increased and
b) decreased?

27 Why do the two food chains considered here produce different pyramids of numbers?

28 Why do you think there are usually more organisms at the bottom of a food chain?

Not all pyramids of numbers are widest at the base. For example, a tree creeper is a small brown bird with a narrow beak that feeds on insects that in turn feed on an oak tree. The food chain of this feeding relationship is:

oak tree → insects → tree creeper

When the food chain is studied further and a pyramid of numbers is displayed it appears as shown in Figure 11.19.

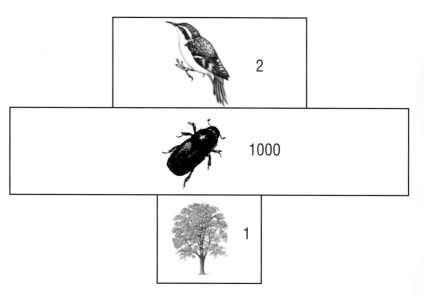

Figure 11.19 Pyramid of numbers of oak tree, insects and tree creepers.

Pyramid of biomass
The amount of matter in a body is found by drying it to remove all water then weighing it. This amount of matter is called the biomass. Ecologists find measuring biomass useful as it tells them how much matter is locked up in each species of a food chain.

Food webs

When several food chains are studied in the habitat some species may appear in more than one. For example, a badger eats blackberries and also eats snails. The two food chains it appears in are:

blackberry → badger
plant → snail → badger

The two food chains can then be linked together as:

blackberry → badger
↗
plant → snail

29 Living things need water in their bodies to survive. What happens to the living things used to work out a pyramid of biomass? Explain your answer.

30 If you drew a pyramid of biomass for the food chain

oak tree → insects → tree creeper

what do you think it would look like? How would it compare to the pyramid of numbers? Explain any differences that you would see.

When all the food chains in a habitat are linked up they make a food web.

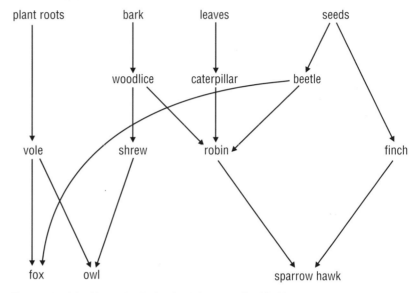

Figure 11.20 Example of a food web in a woodland habitat.

31 How may the numbers of other species in the wood change if each of the following species were removed in turn:
a) fox
b) sparrow hawk
c) beetle?

A poison in the food chain

In 1935 Paul Müller set up a research programme to find a substance that would kill insects but would not harm other animals. Insects were his target because some species are plant pests and devastate farm crops and others carry microbes that cause disease in humans. The substance also had to be cheap to make and not have an unpleasant smell. In 1939 he tried a chemical called dichlorodiphenyltrichloroethane, usually called DDT, that was first made in 1873. DDT seemed to meet all his requirements and soon it was being made in large amounts and used worldwide.

In time, some animals at the end of the food chains (the top carnivores) in the habitats where DDT had been sprayed to kill insects were found dead. The concentration of the DDT applied to the insects was much too weak to kill the top carnivores directly so investigations into the food chains had to be made.

In Clear Lake, California, DDT had been sprayed onto the water to kill gnat larvae. The concentration of DDT in the water was only 0.015 parts per million (ppm), but the concentration in the dead bodies of the grebes (fish-eating water birds) was 1600 ppm. When the planktonic organisms were examined their bodies contained 5 ppm and the small fish that fed on them contained 10 ppm.

32 Construct the food chain investigated in Clear Lake.
33 Why did the grebes die?

It was discovered that DDT did not break down in the environment but was taken into living tissue and stayed there. As the plankton in the lake were eaten by the fish the DDT was taken into the fishes' bodies and built-up after every meal. The small fish were eaten by larger fish in which the DDT formed higher concentrations still. The grebes ate the large fish and with every meal increased the amount of DDT in their bodies until it killed them.

In Britain, the peregrine falcon is a top carnivore in a food chain in moorland habitats, although it visits other habitats outside the breeding season. The concentration of DDT in the bodies of the female falcons caused them to lay eggs with weak shells. When the parents incubated the eggs their weight broke the shells and the embryos in the eggs died.

Habitat destruction

The first humans did not destroy habitats. They hunted animals and gathered plants to eat in the same way that a few groups of people in the rainforests still do today. When people discovered how to raise crops and farm animals the size of the human population began to rise slightly as there was more food to eat.

In the last few hundred years the size of the human population has grown rapidly as people become healthier, live longer and produce more children. Towns and cities have been set up and habitats destroyed to provide the space for them and the farm land needed to support them. Today, with a human population of about 6 billion and still rising, habitats are being destroyed every moment of the day to provide extra room. Tropical rainforests are being destroyed at the rate of an area the size of a football pitch every second to make room for farms, roads and towns.

Figure A Habitat destruction caused by building a road.

(continued)

Woodlands are being destroyed to make space for roads, houses and factories. Hedgerows have been removed to make larger fields for growing crops. Freshwater habitats such as lakes and rivers have been polluted with sewage and industrial wastes. These pollutants have also been released into the sea where marine habitats are also at risk from oil pollution from shipwrecked tankers.

Power stations provide electricity. This makes our lives easier but acid rain caused by power station smoke has destroyed forests and polluted lakes and rivers. The carbon dioxide produced by burning coal and oil in power stations adds to the greenhouse effect and leads to global warming. Carbon dioxide in the atmosphere acts like glass in a greenhouse. It lets heat energy from the Sun pass through it to the Earth's surface but it does not let heat from the Earth's surface pass through the atmosphere into space. The heat is trapped in the atmosphere and causes the temperature of the atmosphere to rise. Without this rise in temperature the Earth would be too cold for living things to survive.

Adding more and more carbon dioxide to the atmosphere leads to an increased temperature. This is called global warming and leads to a melting of the polar ice, a raising of the sea-level and changes in climate in all places on the planet.

Power stations that use nuclear energy do not produce gases that add to the greenhouse effect and global warming. However, they do present the risk of the leak of radioactive materials. The radiation from these materials can destroy any kind of habitat.

Fertilisers increase the amount of food that can be grown and make it cheaper. But the use of too much fertiliser has meant that some of it drains into freshwater habitats and can cause an overgrowth of algae. When the algae die back large numbers of bacteria develop to decompose them. The bacteria use up so much oxygen from the water that other forms of water life suffocate and die.

More food, more living space, more electrical energy, more fuel for vehicles, more materials to use in a wide range of ways have improved the quality of life for millions of people. But in order to provide all of these things habitats have had to be removed. In the past, when the human population was small, the scale of habitat destruction was also small. Today, with a huge human population, the scale of habitat destruction is vast. Many people feel that more care should be taken in balancing the needs of humans with the destruction of the remaining natural habitats. In many countries there are laws that protect some habitats from destruction and therefore any changes to the remaining habitats have to be carefully planned.

Figure B   An oil-polluted beach.

1   Why do habitats have to be cleared?
2   How have habitats been destroyed by other forms of human activity?
3   Try to imagine the lifestyle of the early humans who hunted animals and gathered plants. Compare this lifestyle with your own. What would you change in your own lifestyle to prevent habitat destruction?

Figure C   A freshwater habitat polluted by fertiliser.

(continued)

4 Figure C shows the position of two coastal towns.

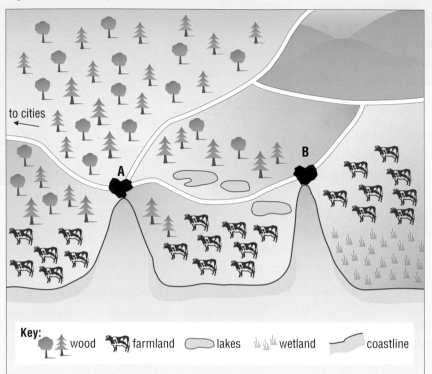

Key:
🌲 wood   🐄 farmland   ⬭ lakes   〰 wetland   ⌇ coastline

Figure C Map showing positions of towns A and B.

A and B are two towns that have a fishing industry. Due to over-fishing the industry has declined. There are large numbers of people now unemployed in both towns and many are thinking of moving or travelling to the cities to find work. It is proposed to build an oil refinery near one of the towns. This will bring employment for the people in the form of building and running the refinery, and in the factories that may be set up to use its products. Land will be needed for the refinery and for the port where the oil tankers will dock. Land will also be needed for factories and perhaps housing estates if more people come to live in the town.

a) What else may land be needed for if more people come to the town?

b) What habitats may be affected by the building of the oil refinery? Explain your answers.

> *For discussion*
>
> **What are the advantages and disadvantages of choosing to build the refinery near town A or B?**
>
> **What are the major issues involved in deciding where the refinery is to be built?**
>
> **How would you balance these issues to decide which town is best suited for the refinery and the port?**

Decomposers

Figure 11.21   These Malaysian termites are feeding on leaf litter.

Not only do the living bodies of each species provide food for others but their dead bodies and wastes are food too. The dead bodies of plants and animals are food for fungi, bacteria and small invertebrates that live in the soil and leaf litter. These organisms are called decomposers. When they have finished feeding, the bodies of plants and animals become reduced to the substances from which they were made. For example, the carbohydrates in a plant are broken down to carbon dioxide and water as the decomposers respire. Other substances are released from the plant's body as minerals and return to the soil. Decomposers are recyclers. They recycle the substances from which living things are made so that they can be used again.

34 Why are decomposers important? How do they affect you?

Ecosystems

Decomposers form one of the links between the living things in a community and the non-living environment. Green plants form the second link. When a community of living things, such as those that make up a wood, interact with the non-living environment – the decomposers releasing minerals, carbon dioxide and water into the environment and then plants taking them in again – the living and non-living parts form an ecological system or ecosystem. An ecosystem can be quite small, such as a pond, or as large as a lake or a forest.

Working out how everything interacts is very complicated but is essential to ecologists (scientists who study ecosystems) if they are to understand how each species in the ecosystem survives and how it affects other species and the non-living part of the ecosystem. Figure 11.22 shows how the living and non-living parts of a very simple ecosystem react together.

35 How might studying ecosystems help to conserve endangered species?

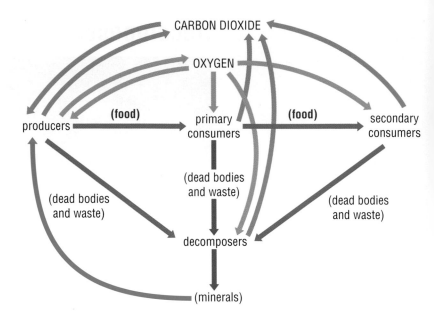

Figure 11.22   Some relationships in a simple ecosystem.

36 An aquarium tank set up with pond life is an ecosystem.
See Figure 11.23.

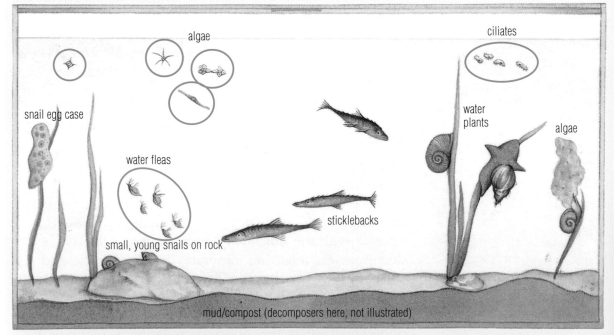

Figure 11.23   An aquarium with pond life. The circled organisms are greatly magnified.

    a) Which are the producers and which are the consumers?

    b) Construct some food chains that might occur in the tank.

    c) Where are the decomposers?

    d) Give examples of the ways the living things react to their non-living environment.

Indicators of pollution

Some living things are very sensitive to pollution and therefore can be used as biological indicators of pollution.

Lichens (see page 182) are sensitive to air pollution. Where the air is very badly polluted no lichens grow but a bright green Protoctista called *Pleurococcus* may form a coating on trees. Crusty lichens, some species of which are yellow, can grow in air where there is some pollution. Leafy lichens grow where the air has only a little pollution. Bushy lichens can only grow in unpolluted air.

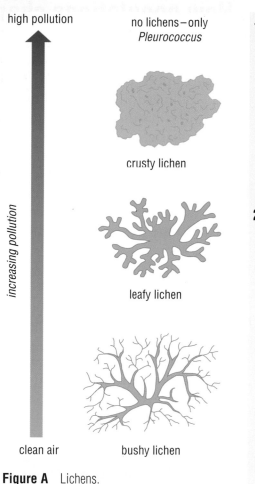

high pollution

no lichens – only *Pleurococcus*

crusty lichen

increasing pollution

leafy lichen

clean air

bushy lichen

Figure A Lichens.

1 How polluted is the habitat if:
  a) the trees have *Pleurococcus* and crusty yellow lichens on them?
  b) bushy, leafy and crusty lichens are found in a habitat?
  c) freshwater shrimps and bloodworms are found in a stream?

2 Four places were examined in succession along a river and the animals found there were recorded. Here are the results.
  A) Stonefly nymphs, mayfly nymphs, freshwater shrimp, caddis-fly larvae.
  B) Rat-tailed maggots, sludge worms.
  C) Sludge worms, bloodworms, waterlouse.
  D) Freshwater shrimps, waterlouse.
  What do the results show? Explain your answer.

Some freshwater invertebrates can be used to estimate the amount of pollution in streams and rivers. If the water is very badly polluted there is no freshwater life but if the water is quite badly polluted rat-tailed maggots may be present. Bloodworms can live in less badly polluted water and freshwater shrimps can live in water that has only small amounts of pollution. Stonefly nymphs can only live in unpolluted water.

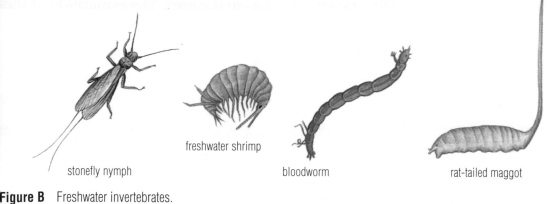

stonefly nymph

freshwater shrimp

bloodworm

rat-tailed maggot

Figure B Freshwater invertebrates.

How populations change

If an area of ground is cleared of vegetation it will soon be colonised by new plants and animals. The following is an account of how an area of soil could be colonised. The colonisation is much simpler than occurs naturally so that the ways the plants and animals interact can be seen more clearly.

A seed lands in the centre of a soil patch and germinates. The plant is an ephemeral and is soon full grown and producing flowers and seeds. The seeds are scattered over the whole area. They all germinate and grow so the population of the ephemeral plants increases.

There are perennial plants outside the area of cleared soil that have stems with broad leaves that cover the ground. As the population of the ephemeral plants increases the perennial plants grow into the area of cleared soil. The two kinds of plants compete for light, water and minerals in the soil. As the numbers of both plants increase the competition between them also increases. The perennials compete more successfully for the resources in the habitat than the ephemeral plants and produce more offspring. The broad leaves of the perennial plants cover the soil and prevent seeds from landing there and germinating. The leaves may also grow over the young ephemeral seedlings. In time the ephemeral plants that are producing seed will die and the stems and broad leaves of the perennials could cover them too.

Herbivorous insects land on some of the perennial plants and start to feed on their leaves. They feed and breed and as their numbers increase they spread out over other perennial plants in the area. The population of the perennial plants in the area begins to fall and the population of ephemerals, which are not eaten by the insects, begins to rise.

A few carnivorous insects land in the centre of the patch. They clamber about on the plants and feed on the herbivorous insects. The well-fed carnivorous insects breed and their population increases. The population of the herbivorous insects starts to fall.

37 In what ways do the two kinds of plants compete for the resources?

38 If the herbivorous insects had not arrived what do you think would have happened to the two populations of plants?

39 How did the arrival of the herbivorous insects affect your prediction in question 38? Explain your answer.

40 What effect do the carnivorous insects have on the population of **a)** herbivorous insects and **b)** ephemeral plants?

41 How may the population of herbivorous insects change over a period of time?

42 Draw a freehand graph to show the change in size of the population of **a)** herbivorous insects and **b)** carnivorous insects over time.

Predicting changes in populations

The changing size of the human population can be predicted by comparing birth rates with death rates. The birth rate is the number of babies born per 1000 people in the population in a year. The death rate is the number of people dying per 1000 people in the population in a year.

If the birth rate is greater than the death rate the population will increase in size. If the death rate is greater than the birth rate the population will decrease in size. If the birth rate and the death rate are the same the population will remain unchanged.

Birth rates, death rates and conservation

Many endangered mammal species have been reduced to a small world population by hunting. The animals have been killed faster than they can reproduce. If the death rate exceeds the birth rate the mammal species is set on a course for extinction. Many mammals are now threatened with this course.

They can be helped by raising their birth rate and reducing their death rate. Zoos can help increase the size of the world population of some endangered animal species. They do this by increasing the birth rate by making all the adult animals in their care healthy enough to breed and by providing extra care in the rearing of the young. Zoos also reduce the death rate by protecting the animals from predation. In many countries reserves have been set up in which endangered animals live naturally but are protected from hunting by humans. This reduces the death rate, which in turn increases the birth rate as more animals survive to reach maturity and breed.

For discussion

Large mammals need large areas of natural habitat to support a large population. With the increasing human population why is it difficult to conserve these large areas? Explain your answer.

Figure 11.24   A Java rhinoceros which is threatened with extinction.

Biomes

If a piece of ground is cleared and left to be colonised by plants and animals a community will develop that is suited to the climate and the underlying soil. If land was cleared in many places of the United Kingdom it would be colonised by ephemeral plants, then grass, and eventually bushes and trees until a deciduous woodland or forest formed. This is the community that is best suited to the environmental conditions and it would remain as long as the conditions prevailed or if there was no interference from humans. This type of community is capable of forming over many thousands of square miles of the United Kingdom and Europe where the land experiences a temperate climate. It is called a temperate forest biome. In other parts of the world there are other biomes. The major ones are the tropical rainforest, desert, and grasslands such as the savannah in Africa.

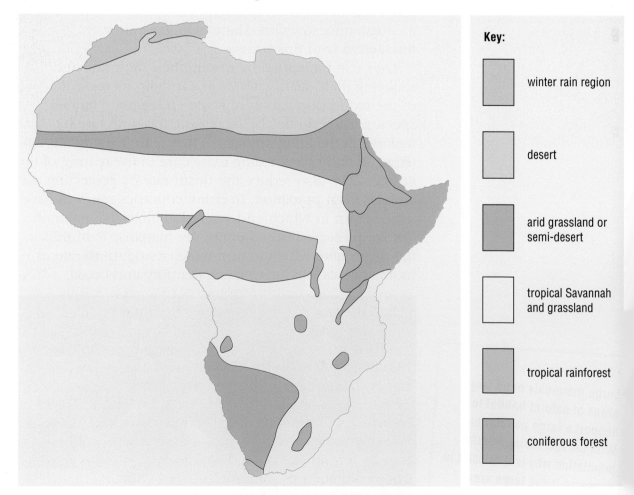

Key:

winter rain region

desert

arid grassland or semi-desert

tropical Savannah and grassland

tropical rainforest

coniferous forest

Figure 11.25 The biomes of Africa.

Communities in the ocean

Most of the planet is covered by oceans. The main regions of the oceans in which different living things are found are the shores, the sea floor around continents, the open sea (down to the point at which all light is absorbed) the dark open waters, and the floors of the deep ocean below 6000 m.

Figure 11.26   A coral reef community.

Biosphere

The biomes on land and the different regions of the oceans where communities of living things exist contain numerous ecosystems. All these ecosystems make a layer of living things over the surface of the planet. This is called the biosphere. It stretches from the ocean depths to high into the air.

When space scientists began devising tests to search for life on other planets they noticed that, generally, life forms change their own environment by the things they take from it and the wastes they release into it. These studies led to the idea that a planet with life on it would have a very different environment to what would be expected from the general conditions in the Universe. They compared the atmosphere and temperature of the Earth with Mars and Venus and also compared a model of the Earth without life with the three planets. They discovered how similar the Earth model was to Mars and Venus, and how different the real Earth was from the other three. This led some scientists to think that living things had created their own environment to allow them to survive.

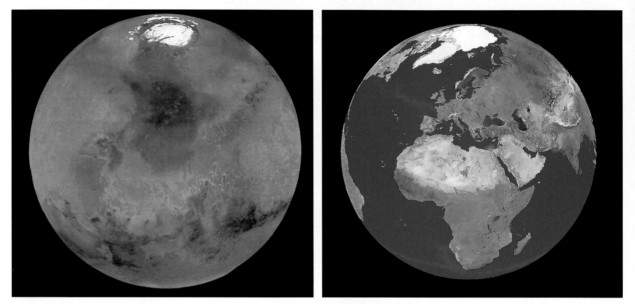

Figure 11.27   Mars (left) and Earth (right).

They took the idea further by considering the length of time life had been on the Earth and how it had coped with the possible life-threatening changes that may have taken place. Fossils show that there has been life on Earth for at least 3.6 billion years. During that time it is known that the radiation from the Sun has varied and that large asteroids have hit the Earth. If life has been able to survive despite these changes the scientists reasoned that the living things on the planet must have regulated themselves to cope. This idea has led to the Gaia Hypothesis, put forward by James E. Lovelock (1919–), in which the biosphere is thought to act like a living thing and adapt to changes. Not everyone agrees with this hypothesis but most people would probably agree that in the last two centuries humans have become as life threatening to the biosphere as any other events that have happened in the Earth's history.

43 What is the difference between a biome and the biosphere?

44 What is the relationship between a biome and the biosphere?

45 What are the major threats produced by humans to the biosphere?

◆ SUMMARY ◆

◆ There are abiotic and biotic factors in a habitat which affect living things (*see page 169*).

◆ Plant distribution can be examined using a quadrat and by making a transect (*see pages 169 and 170*).

◆ The Tullgren funnel, pitfall trap, sweep net, sheet and beater can be used to investigate small animals in land habitats (*see pages 172–174*).

◆ A small range of nets may be used to collect small animals from aquatic habitats (*see pages 174–175*).

◆ Living things survive in their habitats because of adaptations that allow them to survive in the conditions there (*see page 175*).

◆ Some small animals can be kept in the laboratory and their behaviour can be studied by using harmless experiments (*see page 180*).

◆ A food chain shows how plants and animals are related through feeding (*see page 182*).

◆ A pyramid of numbers shows the numbers of each species at each link in the food chain (*see page 183*).

◆ Food chains can be linked together to make food webs (*see page 184*).

◆ Poisonous materials can be concentrated in the bodies of living things in a food chain (*see page 185*).

◆ Decomposers break down the dead bodies and wastes of living things into simple substances (*see page 189*).

◆ The living and non-living parts of a habitat form an ecosystem (*see page 189*).

◆ Populations change due to competition, predation and adaptation (*see page 192*).

◆ Birth rates and death rates are important in predicting changes in populations (*see page 193*).

◆ A biosphere is a layer of living things that covers the surface of a planet (*see page 195*).

End of chapter questions

1 How would you set about investigating a habitat such as a hedgerow?

2 What surfaces do river limpets prefer? The river limpet lives in fast-flowing streams and rivers. There are many different surfaces on the bottom of a stream or river. This experiment was devised to test the results of observations in streams and rivers. The experiment also tested limpets of different sizes to see if larger ones had different preferences to smaller ones.

A 9 cm crystallising dish was divided into four sections called sectors. Each sector had one type of material, either sand, grit, stone or glass. The sectors were covered with water. Twelve limpets were used in each trial and there were two trials for each size class. New limpets were used for each trial. During each trial the number of limpets in each section was recorded after 30 minutes and 60 minutes. The results are displayed in Table 11.2.

(continued)

Table 11.2

Size class/ mm	30 minutes						60 minutes					
	Sand	Grit	Stone	Glass	Total Rough	Total Smooth	Sand	Grit	Stone	Glass	Total Rough	Total Smooth
3–4	5	1	9	9	6	18	3	0	15	6	3	21
4–5	1	1	17	5	2	22	0	0	19	5	0	24
5–6	1	1	17	5	2	22	0	0	20	4	0	24
6–7	2	3	11	8	5	19	0	0	21	3	0	24
Total	9	6	54	27	15	81	3	0	75	18	3	93

a) How many
 i) size classes were there
 ii) trials were made in total
 iii) limpets took part in the experiment?

b) After 30 minutes what can you conclude about the surface the limpets preferred?

c) What has happened in the crystallising dish during the period from 30 to 60 minutes?

d) What can you conclude about the limpets' surface preferences?

e) Do different sized limpets have different surface preferences?

f) A limpet has a foot like a snail or slug. Why do you think it prefers the surfaces shown in the results?

g) If the experiment was extended to 2 hours what results would you predict?

3 The tufted hair grass forms a clump called a tussock. This provides a habitat for different kinds of invertebrates. The numbers of individuals of the different kinds of invertebrates were investigated over an 8-month period.

 Fifteen tussocks were dug up at random on a common each month and were taken apart carefully. The animals in each tussock were collected, arranged into groups and counted. The graphs in Figure 11.28 were produced from the data collected.

a) How did the numbers of butterflies and moths (larvae and pupae) change during the 8 months?

b) Describe the population of animals in the tussocks in April.

c) How did the population change by May?

d) Why were the tussocks picked at random?

(continued)

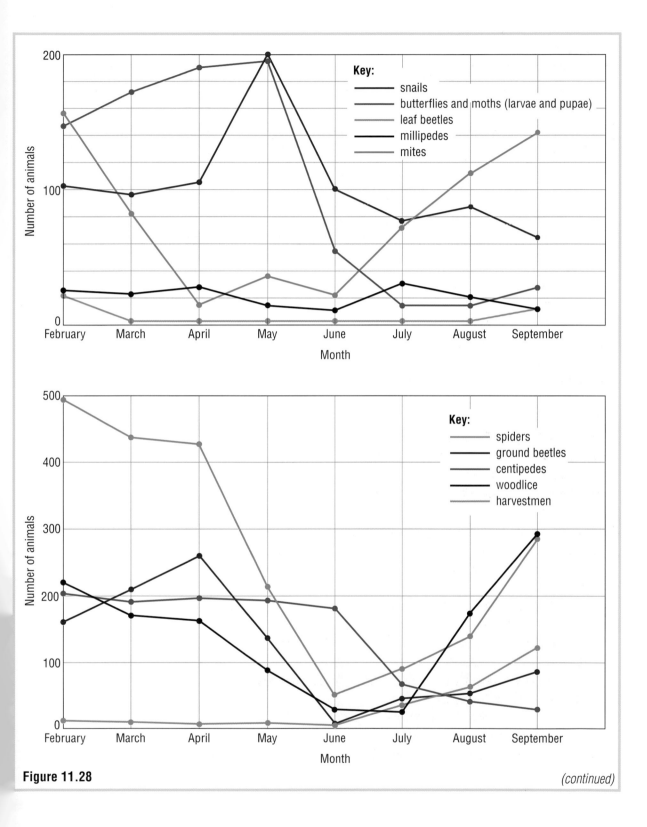

Figure 11.28

(continued)

The animals found in the tussocks of tufted hair grass were compared with those in the tussocks of cocksfoot grass in May. The results were displayed in a bar chart (Figure 11.29).

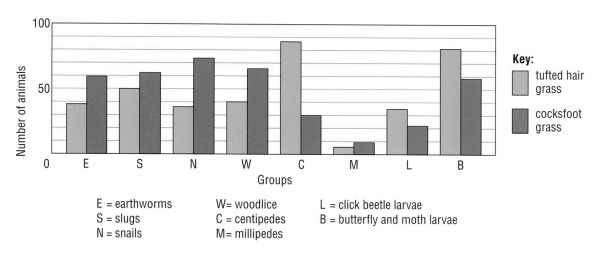

E = earthworms
S = slugs
N = snails

W= woodlice
C = centipedes
M= millipedes

L = click beetle larvae
B = butterfly and moth larvae

Figure 11.29

e) What are the two most numerous groups of animals in
   i) the tufted hair grass tussocks
   ii) the cocksfoot tussocks?
f) Which group of animals is found almost in the same numbers in both tussocks?
g) Which group of animals is twice as numerous in one type of tussock compared to the other?

The animals found in the tussocks of the cocksfoot grass in June were compared with those found in a rush tussock. The two pie charts in Figure 11.30 show how the populations compare.

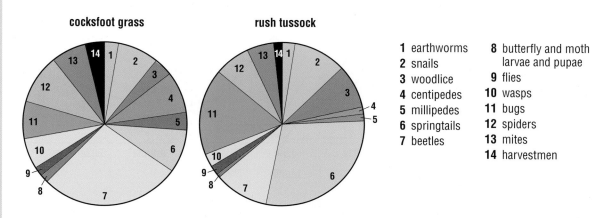

1 earthworms
2 snails
3 woodlice
4 centipedes
5 millipedes
6 springtails
7 beetles

8 butterfly and moth
  larvae and pupae
9 flies
10 wasps
11 bugs
12 spiders
13 mites
14 harvestmen

Figure 11.30

h) What are the major ways in which the animal populations in the two tussocks differ?

Glossary

A

adaptation   The way a living thing is suited to its habitat so that it can survive there. Adaptation can also mean the process by which living things become more suited to their habitat.

addiction   A condition in which a person is unable to lead a normal life without taking drugs or alcohol on a regular basis.

adolescence   The time in a person's life when they change from a child to an adult.

aerobic respiration   The release of energy from food using oxygen.

alimentary canal   The digestive tube that begins with the mouth and ends with the anus. It is also sometimes called the gut.

amino acid   A molecule containing carbon, hydrogen, oxygen and nitrogen. It links up with other amino acids to form long chain molecules called proteins.

amnion   A sac that surrounds the embryo that is filled with a watery fluid.

anaemia   An unhealthy condition that may be due to the lack of iron in the diet. One of the symptoms is tiredness.

anaerobic respiration   The release of energy from food without the use of oxygen.

antagonistic muscles   A pair of muscles in which each of the contracting muscles brings about a movement that is opposite in direction to the other.

anther   The organ in a flower that produces pollen grains.

antibiotic   A chemical made by some microbes or produced artificially by chemical reactions that is used to kill certain kinds of disease-causing bacteria.

antibody   A chemical made by some white blood cells to protect the body from disease-causing microbes and their toxins.

antigen   A feature found on the body of a disease-carrying microbe that stimulates the human body to produce antibodies.

artery   A blood vessel with elastic walls that carries blood away from the heart.

asexual reproduction   The process of producing offspring without the making of gametes and the process of fertilisation.

B

bile   A substance made by the liver and stored in the gall bladder. It is released onto food in the duodenum to aid the digestion of fats.

biodegradable   The property of a complex substance that allows it to be broken down into simple substances by the action of decomposers.

biomass   The mass of an organism or group of organisms after their bodies have been dried out.

biome   A community of plants and animals that forms over a large area of land, such as the temperate forest biome in the United Kingdom or the tropical rainforest biome of central Africa.

biosphere   The layer of living things that covers the surface of the planet.

biotechnology   The use of biological processes to make useful substances, such as antibiotics, and to produce new kinds of living organisms through genetic engineering.

C

calyx   The ring of sepals in a flower.

capillary   A blood vessel with one-cell thick walls through which substances pass between the blood and the surrounding cells.

carbohydrate   A nutrient made from carbon, hydrogen and oxygen. Most are made by plants.

carnivore   An animal that only eats other animals for food.

carpel   The female organ of a flower that produces the fruit and the seed.

cell (in biology)   The basic unit of life. The cell contains a nucleus, cytoplasm and membrane around the outside. The bodies of most living things are made from large numbers of cells.

chlorophyll   A green pigment found mainly in plant cells that traps energy from sunlight and makes it available for the process of photosynthesis.

chloroplast   A component of a cell. It is green and absorbs some of the energy of sunlight for use in photosynthesis.

chromosome   A thread-like structure that appears when the cell nucleus divides. It contains DNA.

cilia   Short hair-like projections that may form on the surface of a cell. They can beat to and fro to move the bodies of Protoctistas or to help with the movement of fluids in animal systems.

clone One of a number of identical individuals produced by asexual reproduction.

consumer An animal that eats either plants or other animals.

contraception The prevention of the development of an embryo.

corolla The ring of petals in a flower.

cross-pollination The transfer of pollen from the anthers of a flower on one plant to the stigma of a flower on another plant of the same species.

cytoplasm A fluid-like substance in the cell in which processes take place to keep the cell alive.

D

digestion The process of breaking down large food particles into small ones so that they can be absorbed by the body.

DNA (deoxyribonucleic acid) A substance in the nuclei of cells that contains information, in the form of a code, about how an organism should develop and function.

E

ecology The study of living things in their natural surroundings or habitats.

ecosystem An ecological system in which the different species in a community react with each other and with the non-living environment. Ecosystems are found in all habitats such as lakes and woods.

egestion (*see also* excretion) The release of undigested food and other contents of the alimentary canal from the anus.

embryo The body of an organism in its early development from a zygote (*see also* zygote). In humans an embryo develops in the womb in the first 2 months of pregnancy (*see also* fetus).

endoskeleton A skeleton on the inside of the body, as occurs in vertebrates.

enzyme A chemical made by a cell that is used to speed up chemical reactions in life processes such as digestion and respiration.

evolution The process by which one species of living thing is believed to change genetically over a period of time in order to develop into a more complex organism.

excretion (*see also* egestion) The release of waste products made by chemical reactions inside the body.

exoskeleton A skeleton on the outside of the body, as occurs in arthropods.

F

fats Food substances that provide energy. They belong to a group of substances called lipids, which include oils and waxes.

fermentation A type of anaerobic respiration that occurs in yeast and bacteria. Some fermentation processes are used to make alcohol.

fertilisation The fusion of the nuclei from the male and female gametes that results in the formation of a zygote.

fetus A stage in the development of the mammal in the womb when the main features of the animal have formed. In humans the fetus develops in the womb from the 2nd to the 9th month of pregnancy.

fruit A structure that forms from the ovary of a flowering plant after fertilisation has taken place.

G

gamete A cell involved in sexual reproduction, i.e. a sperm or egg cell in animals.

gene A section of DNA that contains the information about how a particular characteristic, such as hair colour or eye colour, can develop in the organism.

genetic engineering The process of moving genes between different types of organisms to produce new organisms with particularly useful properties.

germination The process in which the plant inside a seed begins to grow and bursts out of the seed coat.

gonadotrophin A chemical produced by the pituitary gland that stimulates the reproductive organs of males and females to develop fully.

growth hormone A chemical produced by the pituitary gland in the head. It makes the body grow.

H

habitat The place where a particular living thing survives.

haemoglobin The pigment in red blood cells that contains iron and transports oxygen around the body.

herbivore An animal that eats only plants for food.

hormone A chemical, secreted by a gland in the body, which travels in the blood and acts on particular parts of the body. It may produce changes in growth or activity.

hygiene   The study and practice of maintaining health by keeping the body clean.

I

immunisation   A process in which the body is made resistant or immune to a disease.

incubation   A process in which organisms, such as a developing chick in an egg or colonies of bacteria, are kept at a constant, raised temperature to aid their growth and development.

invertebrate   An animal that does not have a skeleton of cartilage or bone inside its body.

J

joint   A place where two bones meet. In movable joints the bones are held together by ligaments and are capped in cartilage to reduce friction.

L

lymphocyte   A white blood cell that makes antibodies to destroy bacteria.

M

menopause   The time in a woman's life, usually about the age of 50, when monthly periods (menstruation) stops.

menstruation   A period of time each month when the uterus loses the lining of its wall.

milk teeth   The first set of teeth that grows in the jaws of young mammals, including humans.

mineral (in biology)   A substance taken up in the soil water by the plant roots and used for growth and development of the plant. It is also an essential nutrient in the diet of animals.

mutation   A change in a gene or chromosome that occurs suddenly and produces a change in the development of the organism.

N

natural selection   The process by which evolution is thought to take place. Individuals in a species best suited to an environment will thrive there and produce more offspring, while less well-suited individuals will produce fewer offspring. In time the less well-suited will die out leaving the best suited individuals to form a new species.

nucleus (in biology)   The part of the cell that contains the DNA and controls the activities and development of the cell.

nutrient   A substance in a food that provides a living thing with material for growth, development and good health.

O

omnivore   An animal that eats both plants and animals for food.

organ   A part of the body, made from a group of cell tissues, that performs an important function in the life of the organism.

ovary   The organ where the female gametes are made in plants and animals.

P

peristalsis   The wave of muscular contraction that moves food along the alimentary canal.

phloem   A living tissue in a plant through which food made in the leaves passes to all parts of the plant.

photosynthesis   The process by which plants make carbohydrates and oxygen from water and carbon dioxide, using the energy from light that has been trapped in chlorophyll.

pistil   A structure made from a group of carpels.

placenta   A disc of tissue that is connected to the uterus wall and supplies the baby with oxygen and food from the mother's blood and releases waste from the baby into the mother's circulatory system.

plankton   Very small (including microscopic) organisms that live near the water surface in large aquatic environments such as oceans and lakes.

pollen   Microscopic grains produced by the anther, which contain the male gamete for sexual reproduction in flowering plants.

pollination   The transfer of pollen from an anther to a stigma.

protein   A substance made from amino acids. Proteins are used to build many structures in the bodies of living things.

puberty   The time of body growth in humans during which the reproductive organs become fully developed.

R

reflex   An action that can take place in the body without using the thought processes in the brain.

respiration   The process in which energy is released from food.

S

saliva A watery substance produced by glands in the mouth that makes food easier to swallow and begins the digestion of carbohydrates.

seed A structure that forms from the ovule after fertilisation. It contains the embryo plant and a food store.

self-pollination The transfer of pollen from the anthers to the stigma of the same flower.

sepal A leaf-like structure that protects a flower when it is in bud.

sexual reproduction The form of reproduction in which gametes are formed, fertilisation takes place and a zygote is formed.

spore A reproductive structure, containing one or more reproductive cells, produced by fungi and plants, such as mosses and ferns, that do not produce seeds. They are also produced by bacteria so that they can survive harsh environmental conditions.

stamen A structure in a flower composed of the anther and the filament.

stigma The region on a carpel on which pollen grains are trapped.

stimulus A change in the environment that alters the activity of a living thing.

T

testes The male reproductive organs in animals. They produce sperm.

tissue A structure made from large numbers of one type of cell.

toxins Poisons produced by bacteria which cause disease.

U

urea A chemical made when amino acids are broken down in the body to make a carbohydrate called glycogen. It is excreted by the kidneys.

ureter The tube connecting the kidney to the bladder, through which urine flows.

urethra The tube connecting the bladder to the outside, through which urine passes. In males sperm also pass along this tube.

urine A watery solution that contains urea.

uterus The female organ in which the embryo and fetus develop. It is also known as the womb in humans.

V

vaccine A substance that promotes the production of antibodies to protect the body from certain diseases.

vacuole A large cavity in a plant cell that is filled with a watery solution called cell sap. May also occur as small, fluid-filled cavities in some animal cells and some Protoctistas.

variation A feature that varies among individuals of the same species, such as height or hair colour.

vein A thin-walled blood vessel that transports blood towards the heart.

vertebrate An animal that has a skeleton inside its body made of cartilage or bone.

vitamin A substance made by plants and animals that is an essential component of the diet to keep the body in good health.

X

xylem The non-living tissue in a plant through which the water and minerals pass from the root through to the shoot.

Z

zygote The cell produced after fertilisation has occurred. It divides, grows and eventually forms a new individual.

Index